ADMINISTRATION OF JUSTICE IN THE KHASI HILLS

ADMINISTRATION OF JUSTICE IN THE KHASI HILLS

ERBANORIS JYRWA

AKANSHA PUBLISHING HOUSE
NEW DELHI-110002

AKANSHA PUBLISHING HOUSE
4649-B/21, Ansari Road
Darya Ganj, New Delhi - 110 002
Email: ektabooks@yahoo.com
Ph.: 23263193/9811582579
Fax : 011-23263193

ADMINISTRATION OF JUSTICE IN THE KHASI HILLS

First Published 2006

ISBN 81-8370-051-9

PRINTED IN INDIA

Published by M.P. Misra for Akansha Publishing House, New Delhi and Printed at Tarun Offset Press, Delhi

DEDICATED TO MY DEAR PARENTS

Shoshindro Marbaniang

&

Beatris Helen Jyrwa

RAJ BHAVAN
SHILLONG
MEGHALAYA STATE
INDIA

M.M. JACOB
GOVERNOR

FOREWORD

The concept of Law and Justice was a central theme in many of the writings of the early Greek philosophers. According to Plato (B.C. 427—437) in his work on Crime a Moral Error - "In this laws we take action against criminals or simply talk to them we may grant him pleasures or make him suffer. We may know him or disgrace him; fine him or give him gifts. We may use absolutely any means to make him hate injustice and embrace true justice or at any rate, not hate it."

The early concept of a legal system also finds expression in the words of the Greek Law Giver - Salon, who argued that "A community was held together by rewards and penalties"- and the earliest Greek Law codes back him up prescribing punishment on a wide scale.

This book is a commendable attempt by a distinguished scholar, Dr. (Miss) Erbanoris Jyrwa of the North Eastern Hill University to trace the Legal and Judicial system in Khasi Hills since time immemorial. In the British days a legal administrative system developed in this part of the country which was different from that in the rest of the country. IN the administration of justice the local traditional system followed by the tribal people was preserved and the tribals were allowed to administer justice according to their customs.

The author has made a serious study of several facets of the traditional system of administration of Justice in

Khasi Hills. She has traced the evolution of the traditional village council of the Khasi Hills and evaluated the institution of Syiemships in Khasi States as well as the Administration of Justice during the British Rule and after Independence. She has also touched upon the administration of justice in the District Council and conducted a case study of administration of justice in Khasi Hills.

This researched document is a valuable asset and contributes significantly to existing knowledge on the Unique system of administration of Justice in the Khasi Hills existing with the modern legal system.

The legal and administrative system applicable to most of Khasi Hills has changed since Independence. With the introduction of District Councils, by the 6th Schedule of the Constitution of India, after Independence, the Judicial administration in the district was bifurcated between the Deputy Commissioner and the District Councils. In certain matters, the 6th schedule envisages exclusive judicial power by the District Council while in certain other matters the Deputy Commissioners and his Assistants have been entrusted with the exercise of Judicial Power. The powers and functions of local chiefs and traditional organizations were curtailed while on the other hand the District Councils were empowered to constitute village courts and other courts for the trial of suits and cases involving tribal communities within the autonomous areas.

While on the positive side, it can be claimed that the traditional system of administration of Justice has helped to preserve the identity of the tribes and promote dispensation of quick and inexpensive justice, on the negative side, one can say that the system has been too static for too long and has failed to keep pace with the changing times.

Times are changing fast. The Global changes in science, technology, commerce, trade and social intercourse has seen dramatic changes in the last twenty years. As we stand on the threshold of the 21st century, we are looking at a future which is going to be enormously different from anything we have known. We have to prepare ourselves to face the challenges of the present times and be pro-active rather than reactive in our approach. To cite a concrete example from the realm of administration of justice, I may mention that the time has come to consider the separation of the executive and the judiciary in so far as the courts set up by the State are concerned. IN fact as per the recent decision of the Supreme Court, steps for separation of judiciary from the executive are already under way and this has to be taken up expeditiously to carry out justice in a modern democratic state.

The ideas as contained in this book reflects Dr. Jyrwa's experience and detail research on the system of administration of justice as well as hard work under the able guidance and supervision of (Late) Prof. B. Pakem, former Vice-Chancellor of the North Eastern Hill University.

My sincere thanks to Dr. (Miss) Erbanoris Jyrwa for her dedicated work on judicial system in Khasi Hills. I am sure that the contents of this publication and articles thereof will be very useful to all research scholars and others interested in the unique features of traditional justice system of Khasi Hills.

I extend my best wishes to the author and hope that the publication of the book will bring a better appreciation and understanding of the judicial system prevailing in these Hills.

M.M. Jacob
Governor of Meghalaya

PREFACE

The administration of justice in Khasi Hills for a long time was carried on according to customary law. There is no organised system of a police administration in the governing machinery of the Khasis. The hereditary officials consisting of 'Heads' of the '*Hima*' execute the orders or sentences passed with the help of *Sardars*, village headmen and other recognised village authorities of the village concerned where the culprits belonged. The codes of civil and criminal procedure were not introduced. The administrator observed the spirit of these codes.

When the British assumed sovereignty over the Khasi land these indigenous organisations were not swept away. The British took advantage of their existence and the authority of the *Syiems* were recognised through *Sanads*. The policy of the British made the people unaware of the changes in their old-age customs and institutions.

Under the British Raj, the Khasi and Jaintia Hills was divided into two parts– "Khasi and Jaintia Hills District" and "Khasi States". The "Khasi States" one of the Indian States that acceded to the Dominion of India are not parts of British India. In so far as the administration of justice is concerned, the administration for the Khasi and Jaintia Hills District was governed by the Rules of the administration of justice and police prescribed by the Governor.

The Administration of Justice in Khasi Hills is a revised version of only one chapter of a thesis submitted to the North-Eastern Hill University in 1991. Basically, the book is on the judicial system in Khasi Hills. In addition, two more chapters have been added on the evolution of the traditional village council of the Khasis and the evolution of the institution of *Syiemships* in Khasi States for a clear understanding and better insights into the managerial, administrative and political system of the Khasis and the changes which have crept in.

The object of this book is to trace the judicial system in Khasi Hills since time immemorial; the changes made by the British on the system; the effect this had on the traditional administrative and judicial functions; the impact British rule had on the powers and functions of the traditional village authorities and the legacy it had left for the Indian government; the laws, rules and regulations laid down when the Constitution of India came into force; changes that took place with the coming into existence of the District Council and also to understand better how far the District Council in Khasi Hills as transitional institutions has been able to administer justice to the tribal people as well as to present the maximum amount of authentic facts and to arrive at conclusions.

In this book eleven (11) representative cases were selected for detailed studies. The factual material for the study are based on the data collected from primary and secondary sources. The primary sources used are official records published and unpublished, archival documents available both in the State Government, District Council offices, Government records, reports of the Committees and Commissions, discussions with people, eminent scholars and also through interviews with the traditional village authorities, selected *Syiems, Lyngdohs, Sardars* and *Wahadadar* of the twenty five Khasi states, officers of the District Council Court as well as members of the District Council. Bedsides these, secondary sources have also been drawn from books, articles and newspapers. The study of the administration of justice has been made by some scholars and have been written in English in books and articles. A pre-survey of related research work shows that no one has attempted to make an indepth study of the judicial system in Khasi Hills. This study is not only a matter of interest for research, but it will serve as an eye opener for the administrators, officials, non-officials and community at large.

ERBANORIS JYRWA

ACKNOWLEDGEMENTS

I owe a deep sense of gratitude to my supervisor (Late) Prof. B. Pakem, former Vice-Chancellor of NEHU for constant inspiration and able academic guidance that he had all along provided to me for the research work under which had been an active learning process for me.

I gratefully recall my indebtedness to Mr. Laborious Manik Syiem, former *Syiem* of *Hima* Mylliem, Dr. Balajied Singh Syiem, *Syiem of Hima* Khyrim, (Late) Mr. Edwin Lyngdoh, *Lyngdoh* of Mawphlang, Mrs. Dramon Kurbah, Ex-Secretary of the Village Court, Marbisu *Sirdarship*, Mr. H.M. Dkhar, Judge, District Council Court, Mr. J. Reenborn, Additional Judge, District Council Court and Mr. D. Hynñiewta, (Rtd.) Deputy Registrar, Gauhati High Court (Shillong Bench) for extending their kind help and for access to the representative cases at their disposal which were vital for the research work. My grateful thanks are due to them.

I am ever grateful to (Late) Mr. L.G. Shullai for his selfless support, encouragement and the appropriate information which he had extended continuously during his life time. Through fruitful discussion and access to his Shillong Records Collection Centre these enabled me to bring out this research work in its present form.

My sincere thanks and gratitude to all those knowledgeable people for having spared their most valuable time and gave me precious information.

I am most grateful to my dear parents who have always been the greatest support in all my endeavours. I also recall the loving service of my sisters and brothers who always stood by my side in every hour of need.

Lastly, my sincere thanks to the Akansha Publishing House, New Delhi for their acceptance to publish this book and for taking the pain to bring out this book in a very short time.

ERBANORIS JYRWA

CONTENTS

1
INTRODUCTION

According to Tandon Mahesh Prasad, the administration of justice is the maintenance of right within a political community by means of the physical force of the State. It is a device adopted by the modern and civilized community in replacement of the primitive practice of working private vengeance and violent self-help. Further, Tandon stated that the administration of justice is divisible into two parts: (i) Administration of civil justice, and (ii) Administration of criminal justice. Wrongs may either be civil or criminal. The former are dealt with in civil proceedings and the latter in criminal proceedings. The real distinction as observed by the editor of Salmond's 11th edition of Jurisprudence, resides, not in the physical consequence of the act but in its legal consequences by which it may legally be followed.[1]

In the modern state, according to Shambhu Dayal, very often our notion of justice presupposes fixed rules and is incompatible with a system of free judicial discretion. Justice is usually taken to require that people should be treated alike unless there is reason for treating them differently. On the other hand, it cannot be denied that we have some notion of justice independently of legal rules; otherwise we should not be able to consider whether a particular legal rule is just or not.[2] According to Lord Wright, justice is an expression of varying import. It is a multi-flavoured compound. It is very difficult to give a precise and comprehensive definition, which may be acceptable by all. This difficulty was realized by Lord Wright in the following words,

> "I am not afraid of sloppiness of thought when I say that the guiding principle of a judge in deciding cases is to do justice; that is justice according to law, but still justice. I have not found any satisfactory definition of justice ... what is just in any particular case is what appears to be just to be just man, in the same way as what is reasonable is what appears to be reasonable to the reasonable man."[3]

According to Jethro Brow, "justice as a concept of jurisprudence is more conformity to law."[4] For Kelsen, it is simply 'an irrational ideal'. Some take it as the 'equality before law' while others takes it as the 'protection of individual interest'. There are still others who mean by Justice the harmonization of conflicting rights. Anyway "justice is whether I can define it or not".[5]

The administration of Justice in Khasi Hills for a long time was carried on according to customary law. There is no organized system of a police administration in the governing machinery of the Khasis. The hereditary officials consisting of the "Heads" of the "Hima" execute the Orders or sentences passed with the help of *sardars*, village headmen and other recognized village authorities of the village concerned where the culprit belongs. When there is a doubt of resistance the help of the entire village or nearby village is sought, if necessary. The villagers of the respective village come readily to give the assistance when required. These villagers do so in the interest of the security and safety of their own village. The codes of civil and criminal procedure were not introduced into the Khasi Hills. The administrator observed the spirit of these codes.

With the coming of the British in Khasi Hills, the British ruler left the people for sometime almost completely to themselves to lull them in a sense of complacency. The British, however, steadily introduce changes into the traditional system of administration to suit their convenience and also to bring about certain modifications in the traditional institutions to consolidate their positions and strengthen their hold upon the people as their subjects. This policy of the British made the people unaware of the changes in their age-old customs and institutions. Even, the cursory study of the treaties entered with the *Syiems* and the *Sanads* granted to them with one succession after the other reveal the erosion of the powers of the *Syiems*.

Under the British Raj, the Khasi and Jaintia Hills District was divided into two parts: 'Khasi and Jaintia Hills District' and 'Khasi States'. India at that time was divided into three parts viz., 'British India', 'Indian States' and 'Tribal Areas', these tribal areas are not tribal areas as shown in table appended to paragraph 20 of the Sixth Schedule to the Constitution of India. They are tribal areas outside the British India. With the passing of the Indian Independence Act, 1947 by the British Parliament 'British India' was divided into two dominions, that is India and Pakistan, with effect from August 15, 1947. In the North East part of the Dominion of India lays the tribal areas, known as the 'Assam Tribal Areas'. The Assam Tribal Areas become part of the Assam State from January 26, 1950 as given in the First Schedule to the Constitution of India and as passed by the Constituent Assembly of India on November 26, 1949.

The "Khasi States" one of the Indian States that acceded to the Dominion of India are not parts of British India. As per the Government of India Act, 1919, the "Khasi States" need not send the members to the Assam Legislative Council and need not send their members to the Assam Legislative Assembly. As regard the administration of justice in the 'Khasi States' during the British rule, it was administered in accordance with the provisions contained in the *Sanad* issued to the "Heads" (*Syiems, Lyngdohs, Wahadadar* and *Sirdar Hima*) of the Khasi States. The Khasi States were brought within the boundary of an Autonomous District known as the United Khasi-Jaintia Hills Autonomous District vide sub-paragraph (1) of paragraph 20 of the Sixth Schedule to the Constitution of India as originally adopted on the 26 November 1949.

Further, the Khasi and Jaintia Hills District, since they are part of British India they have to send their representatives as per the Government of India Act, 1919. In so far as the administration of justice is concerned, the administration was governed by the Rules for the Administration of Justice and Police in the Khasi and Jaintia Hills prescribed by the Governor in exercise of the powers vested in him by Section 6(six) of the Scheduled District Act, 1874 (Act XIV of 1874) issued under Notification No.2618-A.P. dated the 29 March 1937.

Before 15 August 1947, there was a Central Legislature known as "Indian Legislature" which consists of the Upper House known as "Council of States" and the Lower House known as "Legislative Assembly". For the removal of doubt, it may be mentioned here that the Upper House of the "Indian Legislature" is known as the "Council of State" and the Upper House of the present Parliament of India is known as "Council of States". Besides the "Indian

Legislature" there was a Constituent Assembly which is a Constitution Making Body". The first meetings of the Constituent Assembly of India was held on 9 December 1946. The Government of India Act, 1935 with effect from 15 August 1947 was modified by the India (Provisional Constitution) Order, 1947 promulgated by the Governor General of India as empowered by Section 8 and Section 9 of the Indian Independence Act, 1947 passed by the British Parliament.

The "Indian Legislature" ceased to function with effect from 15 August 1947 and the Constituent Assembly of India assumed both the functions as the "Central Legislature" and as the "Constitution Making Body". The Constituent Assembly (functioning as Central Legislature) on 9 December 1947 passed the Extra Provincial Jurisdiction Act, 1947 which received the assent of the Governor General of India on 24 December 1947. The Constituent Assembly when it sat as a "Constitution Making Body" was presided over by the President (Dr. Rajendra Prasad) and when it sat as a "Central Legislature" was presided over by the Speaker (Shri G.V. Malavankar).[6]

As of now, it may be stated that the traditional Institutions have not been able to play their role in the true sense of their foundation as they were before the British came to interfere with them. Though we do really find such practice in vague among the Khasis, yet whatever might be the situation and forces at work to abolish the customs and traditions we can still find the *Dorbar Shnong, Ka Khang Shnong, Ka Pyrta Shnong,* that play a vital role in the social and political life of the people. The sentiments of the people for the preservation of all the traditional customs can be seen whenever they are made to come into contact with any threat or influence.

Notes and References

1. Tandon, Mahesh Prasad, *Questions and Answers on Jurisprudence (Legal Theory)*, Allahabad Law Agency, Allahabad, 1981, pp.102-103.
2. Dayal, Shambhu, *Jurisprudence and Legal Theory*, Central Law Agency, Allahabad, 1976, pp.110-111.
3. *Ibid.*, p.100.
4. *Ibid.*
5. *Ibid.*
6. Shullai, L.G., "Administration of Justice in Meghalaya", a Paper presented at the Seminar organised by the Law Research Institute, Eastern Region, Guwahati High Court, 4th September, 1999 at the State Central Library, Shillong (unpublished), p.1.

2

EVOLUTION OF THE TRADITIONAL VILLAGE COUNCIL OF THE KHASIS

The story of wherefrom, when and how did the Khasi people migrate to their present abodes is still buried in strict secrecy, mystery and obscurity. It exists only in the world of legends and mythologies, fables and tales, music and songs, and in the world of fantasies and imaginations. This is due to the lack of written records.

Many stories are told that the Khasis came to these hills and dales in search of iron ore, fertile paddy fields and good limestone-bearing slopes for the development of horticulture. When the Khasis came to their present motherland, they did not bring along with them only their personal belongings, as some people might have imagined; but they brought along with them much more, precious legacies. They brought along with them their well-established social system with the most enlightened code of moral conduct and ethical laws, their high political thought and philosophy, their well-organised political system and their deep-rooted religious beliefs. Therefore, the Khasis must have belonged, not to a primitive tribe; but to a highly enlightened civilized and progressive race.

They had the qualities of any civilized race of the then known civilized world. The ideas and ideals and the values that the ancient forebears of the Khasis have not diminished in their dimensions, scales and scopes and their final goals despite the fact that they have passed through many scourges of time and the ravages of interaction. The Khasi people have stood like one solid rock against so many ups and downs of history. It is of this solid foundation that every Khasi sings;

"Khynriam or Pnar or Bhoi or War,
One great people 'Khasi we are'."

In Khasi society, the clan was and is still the unit in the social and political systems of the Khasis. While describing the Khasi social system, David Roy Phanwar observes: "A Khasi places man as the defender of the woman; and the woman as the keeper of his trust". Meantime, while describing the Khasi clanship system, the author concludes: "From the woman springs the kind, the species; it is the father who gives the person the stature; but the words of the maternal uncle are the laws within the clan." To a Khasi, eternal doom and death is preferable to having a thought of loving spiritually and mentally, but not physically outside his own clan.

No single clan could be expected to live and to remain in complete isolation, away from other clans within the confines of its specified occupied and settled area of its jurisdiction. Through the process of intermarriage of its members, males and females, with members of other clan outside the area, new families came up. Again, through the process of goodwill and understanding, other clans came to settle down in other hillocks of the same area. Hence, the structure of population became composite and thus a village came into existence. Each of these clans began to demarcate the boundaries of the arable lands for settlement and use especially for cultivation. These lands, then, became the *Ri-Kynti* or private lands of each particular clan. The right of ownership and occupancy was vested in the whole clan and not to a particular individual. All members of the clan had equal rights to use these private lands. The management of any private land was vested in the hands of the male members of the clan whereas the custodianship of each clan land was vested in the hands of the youngest female members and her family of the clan. Within the private land of the clans, there was *Ka Ri-Shyieng* and the income therefrom was earmarked to spend for religious functions of the clan. There was also *Ka Ri Phniang* inside the private clan land and the income therefrom was set apart by the youngest family in rearing and looking after the orphans and widows and widowers of the clan. All other areas of land, which were not occupied by any clan, belonged to the whole village. They were called *Ri-Shnong* or *Ri-Raid* or commune lands.

Within the confines of the commune lands or lands belonging to the whole village, we find the existence of Green Blocks which were set a part for the conservation of water. One type of these forests was known as *Law Shnong* (Village forest) and the second type was known as *Law Adong* (Reserve forest). No one could be allowed to cut down the trees from the forest, except with the permission of the village council. That also only once a year, and only for building purposes of the villagers, for firewood and for raising funds for the welfare of the whole village. Strict Orders were told by the village council, that once a person cut down the trees, new samplings should be planted so that the areas should not become barren. Beside these protected forests, there were also two other types—one type was known as *Law Kyntang*, or sacred protected forests and the second type was known as *Law Lyngdoh* or sacred forest belonging to the priestly clan of the village. Divine attributes were attached to these forests so that no one could dare even to touch the tiny branch of any tree.

For the purpose of administrative convenience, a village council or *Durbar Shnong* was constituted. The General Assembly consisted of all adult male members of the village. All male members who had full-grown moustache had the right to attend and deliberate in the proceedings of the General Assembly and it's decision making process. Persons who had no moustache, physical deformities and mentally retarded had no right to be present in the General Assembly meeting. Women had no right to attend such meeting. Hence, adult male franchise was the solution.

The executive, administrative and judicial functions of the village were vested in the council of elders. The members of which were to be elected by the General Assembly. The head of this council was known as *Tymmen Shnong* or headman whose duties were to preside over all types of meetings of the council of elders and of the General Assembly. Other members of the council were the *Rangbah Shnong* or head of the localities of the village that were also elected by the General Assembly. There were also advisers who were chosen by the major clans of the village. The main functions of the village councils were to look after the peace and tranquillity of the village, to take proper care of the village commune lands, to look after the water resource and supply, to maintain proper care of footpaths, lanes and bye lanes, market place and the like, to act as a court of judicature when there was any quarrel and also to protect the territory and the people.

The procedure for conducting the administration of

justice was in accordance with the customs handed down from time immemorial. Persuasions and wise counsels of elders more often solved the petty of quarrels. But in major quarrels and boundary dispute or for any civil case, the Council of Elders usually summoned witnesses. The detailed procedure for conducting the administration of justice will be narrated in the foregoing chapters.

The procedure of conducting trials in criminal cases, even in extreme cases of crime was simple. In a village where everyone knew each other very closely. Cases of cheating, theft, robbery and other minor offences and even cases of witchcraft, rape and murder could be easily detected and discovered through simple process of taking evidence from reliable witnesses.

The form of punishment imposed on the losing parties in civil cases and on culprits in criminal cases was numerous. Imposition of fines on losing parties was common. But long period of life imprisonment seemed to be unknown as there is no evidence of the existence of any permanent jail. The forms of punishment according to Khasi law will be discussed in chapter four.

At the beginning, the powers of the village council seemed to be unlimited because it exercised sovereign powers within the areas of its jurisdiction. But with the evolution of the confederacies of village or *Raid* and the final evolution of the *Hima* or State most of the powers of the village Council were taken away by the higher echelons of authorities and the village council lost all its sovereign powers.But in matters concerning adjudication of cases, the *Syiem* and his *Myntries* enjoy only residual powers and the lower units of the State like the *Raid* and villages have been given wider scope. The court of the units also has the power to pass judgement and the *Syiems* court act as the final court of appeal.

Notes and References

1. Bareh, H., *Khasi Democracy*, Ri Khasi Press, Shillong, 1964.
2. Bareh, H., *The History and Culture of the Khasi People*, Shillong, 1967 (Reprinted, Calcutta, 1969)
3. Cantlie, Sir Keith, *Notes on Khasi Law*, A.S. Khongphai (ed.), Shillong, 1974.
4. *Census Reports of India*, 1961. Vol. III, Part VI, No.13.
5. Costa, G., *Ka Jingroi Ka Ri Khasi-1 – Ka Riti Jong Ka Ri Laiphew Syiem.*
6. Costa, G., *Ka Riti Jong ka Ri Laiphew Syiem*: Ka Bynta kaba-ar, Don Bosco Press, Shillong, 1971.
7. Government of India, Ministry of Home Affairs, *Report of the Commission on the Hill Areas of Assam 1965-1966*, Delhi, 1966.
8. Government of Meghalaya, *Report of the Land Reforms Commission for Khasi Hills*, Government Press, Shillong, 1974.
9. Gurdon, P.R.T., *The Khasis*, Macmillan & Co., Ltd., London 1914 (Reprinted, Cosmo Publications, Delhi 1975).
10. Pakem, B., "Political Development and Change in North East India" in A.P. Sinha (ed.), *Changing North East India*, Gagan Publishers, Ludhiana, 1986.
11. Roy, David, *Principles of Khasi Culture*, 1937.
12. Roy, David, *Who is a Khasi?*, 1963.

3

EVOLUTION OF THE INSTITUTION OF SYIEMSHIPS IN KHASI STATES

The evolution of the traditional, social, cultural and political ideals of the Khasis is interwoven round the origin of the Khasi race. The Khasis look upon the *trep* as a *Kur* (clan). Inter-marriage takes place among the different *Kurs* and as a result, those *Kurs* were multiplied in course of time. A *Kur* traced its descent to *Ka Ïawbei Tynrai* or Root Ancestress. With the multiplication of *Kur* and growth of population, the members of some *Kurs* migrated in search of new lands for agriculture, means of livelihood and other facilities. This led to the formation of *Ka Jaid.* The *Jaids* claim to have descended from the common but younger ancestress in the *Kur*, called *Ka Ïawbei Tymmen* or old ancestress. A *Kur* is thus divided into a number of *Jaids.* A *Jaid* is again sub-divided into *Ka Kpoh* which claims descend from *Ka Ïawbei Khynraw* or young ancestress. Each *Kpoh* is sub-divided into *ïng* (houses of families). Through migration, the *Jaid* may be known by a new name but belongs to the same ancestry and the same *Kur.*[1] Thus, the *Kur* was and is still the unit in the social and political system of the Khasis.

The village society could assimilate the members of other *Kurs* who might settle down in the village. The male members of the *Kur* sometimes brought their wives from other *Kurs* to stay in the village, thus increasing the number of *Kurs* in the village. In this way a number of *Kurs* came to stay in the village with only one *Kur*. The founding *Kur* would elect the oldest most intelligent male member to be the ruler of the village. Such a man assumes the office of the *Basan*. The remaining *Kur* in the village also elect their own representatives called *Ki Tymmen ki san* but in a village founded jointly, the minor *Kur* would elect *tymmen shnong* or Headman. There would be one or more headmen in the same village, but all the elected heads whether *Ki tymmen ki san* or *Tymmen shnong* would form a village council with the *Basan*.[2]

Let us now see how the Khasi State or *Syiemship* was formed out of a collection of the clans (*Kur*). With the multiplication of *Kurs*, villages and *Basans*, in course of time, the Khasi States were formed as a result of a mutual agreement among the leaders or *Basans* of the *raids* (commune). Khasi tradition says that "The State was founded on religion" and religion starts with the *Kur*.[3] According to Major Gurdon the Khasi States were formed, in more than one instance, by the voluntary association of villagers, or group of villages. The head of the Khasi States is the *Syiem*. The State was a limited monarchy, the *Syiem's* powers being much circumscribed.[4] Thus, the final stage in the growth, development and evolution of the traditional institutions was the foundation of Khasi States. According to Helen Giri, a combination of factors led to the emergence of Khasi States under the *Syiems*. First, as the villages grew in size and population, the people found it necessary to be under one common administration. The *Syiem* is there not to dictate but to be their philosopher and guide, he would be the mediator between the people and the *Durbar Hima*. In short, the Khasi *Syiems* rule but does not reign. Secondly, it is a popular belief that it is a taboo for the people to administer justice or be incharge of *Ka nar ka bili* or *u Tangon u lymban*, hence the necessity of the *Syiem*. Thirdly, that the *Syiem*, who was ordained by God to come to the earth, has certain super powers to decide between right and wrong, to take charge of *Ka Niam Im Ka Niam ïap* (religion for the living and the dead) of the *Bakhraws* or the people, which the *Bakraws* or the people would regard as a taboo to be brought within their hearth or their clan. Fourthly, as the Khasi States grew in power, strength and influence, there was also every livelihood that they would fall a prey to foreign invasion. The question of defence therefore, demanded the entity of *Syiemship*. Fifthly, the *Basans* of the *Raids* had equal status, there was therefore the necessity of evolving an institution as head of the State.[5]

Mentioned may be made that the Khasis after inherited the land, feels that it should not belong to one person or one group only but everyone has the right to it to govern. On this ground, *Syiemship*, *Lyngdohship* or *Wahadadarship* or *Sirdarship* emerged not by arbitration but by the will and consent of *Ki Khun ki hajar* (children of the soil) of the State concerned on the basis of well established customs and traditions.[6] Now let us see how a Khasi *Syiem* is appointed.

In Khasi States (*Hima Khasi*) the methods of election of the *Syiem* differs from *Syiemship* to *Syiemship* according to custom. Generally speaking, the *Syiem* is appointed from amongst the *Syiems* family. He was elected by an electoral college consisting of the representatives of certain clans which have been in existence by recognised customs. The *Syiem* once appointed cannot be removed from his office unless according to the customs, that it, by means of a referendum of the people. According to custom the *Syiem* could perform no act of any importance without first consulting and obtaining the approval of the *Durbar* upon which the State *Myntries* sat. The *Durbar* was an executive council over which the *Syiem* presided. It had both administrative as well as judicial function. The *Durbar* elects or dethrones the *Syiem*. It gives its assent to the appointment of *Myntries, Lyngdohs* or *Basans*. It decides war and peace and gives its final decision to any suit. Once a *Syiem* is elected he continues in office unless he is otherwise incapable of running the administration of the *Elaka* which render him unfit for holding the office. The *Syiem* managed the State (*Hima*) business through his *myntries* (ministers). The *Syiems* principal source of income, in all the Khasi States was the toll (*Khrong*) which he took from those who sold at the markets within his territory.[7] Sir Keith Contlie in his book *Notes on Khasi Law* laid down that the chiefs in the Khasi Hills States were not territorial sovereigns but elected democratic chiefs whose authority extended over their subjects and not over the lands.[8] Properly speaking, the Khasi *Syiems* could not assert territorial limits, but their jurisdiction extend over villages and the boundaries of such localities constituted the confines of their respective rule.

A Khasi *Syiemship* is unique in its origin. Local traditions maintain that most of the *Syiems* originally were strangers in the land or at least the progenitors of modern *Syiems* did not belong to the original groups of clans. Wanderers from somewhere were often caught and made *Syiems*. This was because *Syiems* were given some exceptional duties which could not be performed by other clans of the society. The main duty of the *Syiems* seems to have been the disposal of the dead bodies of strangers who were clanless in society or to possess some acts of witchcraft. For *Syiems* were supposed to possess some special divine power to counteract sorcery and magic, a power not possessed by others. Another important duty of the *Syiems* was to keep prisoners in their custody as other clans would not accept such services which in public eyes were presumably humiliating.[9]

With regards to the succession of *Syiemship* in Khasi States, the question of succession to *Syiemship* were regulated according to social customs which vary from *Elaka* to *Elaka*. A *Syiem* is normally succeeded by the eldest surviving son of his eldest sister if he is not otherwise disqualified for physical unfitness, moral turpitude or other reasons. If the eldest sister has no son then the son of her next sisters, and in the same manner if the next sister also has no male issue. If the *Syiem* has no uterine sister the succession goes to the sons of his first cousin sisters, the daughter of his mother's sisters, in the same Order and in the like manner. In the event of a failure of succession along the direct line of the late *Syiem's* family (*Kpoh*), the succession is chosen from amongst the male adults who are members of other families belonging to the *Syiem* clan or *Lyngdoh* clan. A well qualified person from such clans is chosen by an electoral college consist of elders who constitutes a *Durbar* which run the day-to-day administration and is termed as the *Syiem's Durbar*, or *Lyngdoh's Durbar*. The elders of each *Hima* (State) are members of select families of the *Hima* holding the title of *Bakhraws* (nobles). The elders from the clans of *Bakhraws* are elected by the male members of their respective clan only. Each clan can send only one representative to the *Syiem's Durbar*.

The number of nobles known as *Myntries* constituting the *Syiem's Durbar* vary from *Hima* to *Hima*. Failing unanimity amongst the members of the Electoral College between them the election of the *Syiem* is thrown open to all the male adults of the *Hima*. When the British occupied the Khasi States they encourage election of a successor from amongst all adult male members of the *Syiem* clan and modified the method of election in some of them by adding certain heads of villages or groups of villages to become member of the electoral college. These members were known as electors. Further, the *Hima* was divided into two category for the ruling convenience. Some were treated as Native States but many others were treated as British territories. In Native States the British recognised the twenty five Khasi States and recognised them into four categories, viz., fifteen of them were of the first class presided over by the *Syiems*, one confederacy under elected officers called *Wahadadars*, five under *Sirdars* and four under *Lyngdohs*. The *Himas* ruled by *Syiems* and *Lyngdohs* were treated by the British as Native States. The *Sirdars* of the Native States were elected from amongst the male members of the select clans. The method of election the *Sirdars* in the Native States is of the same pattern as that in other Native States under the *Syiems* or *Lyngdohs*. The election of a *Sirdar* in British territory is thrown open to all the male adults of the *Sirdarship* concerned.[10]

When the British assumed sovereignty over the land these indigenous organisations were not swept away. The British took advantage of their existence and the authority of the *Syiems* were recognised through *Sanads* granted by the sovereign power. The *Sanad* ratified the appointment of the *Syiem* on his election and he was subject to the control of the Deputy Commissioner of the district of Khasi and Jaintia Hills.[11]

Traditionally, the *Syiem* is not the head of the State

but he is a nominal head. He is a symbol of unity and integrity of the State. It is the *Durbar Hima* which is the paramount power. The *Syiem* is called *u Kmie* which means the mother and therefore guides his people as their mother, nurse and guardian and is concerned with their welfare.. In times of wars, a *Syiem* acted as a commander and while disposing of judicial cases, he acts as the judge. In executive actions, the *Syiem* is constantly advised and assisted by a group of *Myntries* who form his cabinet. The *Syiems* have no powers on their own individual capacity to make laws. A *syiem* has magisterial functions and acts as police officer. A *Syiem* opens the *Durbar* session and the whole business whether it is a piece of legislation or trial of criminals or administrative transactions falls on the body of the *Durbar* in which the whole population or representatives thereof participate.

Notes and References

1. Giri, Helen, *The Khasis under British Rule (1824-1947)*, Akashi Depot, Shillong, 1990, p.10.
2. *Ibid.*, p.14.
3. *Ibid.*, pp.13-15.
4. Gurdon, P.R.T., *The Khasis*, Macmillan & Co., Ltd., London, 1914, Second edition, p.66.
5. Giri, Helen, *op cit.*, p.16.
6. *Ibid.*, p.18.
7. Gurdon, P.R.T., *op cit.*, pp.66-67.
8. Khongphai, A.S. (ed.), *Notes on Khasi Law*, Ri Khasi Press, Shillong, 1947, p.131.
9. Bareh, Hamlet, *Khasi Democracy*, Ri Khasi Press, Shillong, 1964, pp.42-43.
10. Gurdon, P.R.T., *op cit.*, pp.68-72.
11. Khongphai, A.S. (ed.), *op cit.*, pp.138-141.

4

TRADITIONAL SYSTEM OF ADMINISTRATION OF JUSTICE IN KHASI HILLS

Administration of justice in the Khasi Hills can be grouped under two Sections—traditional and modern. The traditional system of administration of justice is confined to the judicial system prevailing today on the pattern devised by traditional rulers in the past. The traditional judicial institution of the Khasis was continued by the British with slight modifications. The Government of free India inherited the system laid down by the forefathers of the Khasis, continued by the British and adopted by the Sovereign Democratic Republic of India.[1]

Before we take a closer look on the administration of justice in the Khasi Hills in the transitional period, Autonomous District Council, it will be worthwhile to take a look at the earlier traditional methods practised by the Khasi people.

Institutions like law courts, judges and legislative bodies are often not found in traditional societies. Social norms were sustained by traditions and no additional authority was needed to maintain them. In Khasi society the authorities that ran the administration or *Ka Synshar*

Ka Khadar were also in charge of judicial matters or *Ka Bishar Ka Khadar*. Further, it was the customs and traditions that were referred to in adjudication as in the case of administration. This procedure has been followed at different levels of State Organisation—*Ka Kyntoit* (locality), *Ka Raid* (commune) and *Ka Hima* (state)

In the olden days, when any one came to lodge a complaint against another person before the *Syiem* or headman, the complainant would be asked if he had any uncle or not, because the complaint should be lodged by them. Secondly, the complainant would be asked if he had any relationship with the accused because if they belonged to the same *Kur* or had any clan relationship, it would involve *Ka Sang Ka Ma* or a taboo. They would then be asked to settle the dispute amicably. If this could not be done, the accused would be asked to appear before the *Syiem* with his or her maternal uncles and families as there were no lawyers, the maternal uncles would plead for the complainant and the accused respectively.[2] Gurdon observes that the ostensible object would be "to bring about a compromise between the parties". If they could not reconcile, the *Durbar Shnong* (local durbar) would be convened.[3]

The administration of justice in the *durbars* of all these customary functionaries is according to what is right, just and in accordance with the custom handed down from time immemorial. People who have a cause go first to the *Rangbah Shnong*. He will then ask them if they have consulted the uncles of their families. If not, he would first send them back to talk with their uncles. If these cannot come to an amicable agreement they would then themselves present the case before the *Rangbah Shnong*. The *Rangbah Shnong* is assisted in the disposal of disputes by a Council of elders chosen by consensus by virtue of their experience, age, knowledge and noted wisdom and integrity. The entire population of male adults of the village or the unit of it sit in *durbar* to decide matters affecting the village or unit as a whole. They also sit as appellate authority to the decision of the *Rangbah Shnong's* council, if called upon.[4]

Appeals from the *Rangbah Shnong's* decision normally go to the *Syiem Raid* or *Lyngdoh Raid* where there is one or directly to the *syiem, lyngdoh, sirdar* where there are no *Raids*. The *durbar* arrives at a decision by way of finding out the truth of the matter by itself if neither of the parties can produce evidence to prove to its satisfaction the undisputable right and authenticity of its claim. In such event, a person known for his neutrality, integrity, impartiality, knowledge of the facts and circumstances of the case and also of the customs and usages governing the people is requested to guide the *durbar*. Such a person is called a *Saiphla* (solicitor or reporter). Alternatively, one party would put it to the other that it is ready and willing to surrender its claim if that party would dare to take a most solemn oath to the effect that its entire family and clan become extinct if its claim is not God's truth. This method or procedure to find out the truth leading to a correct and just decision when all attempts at amicable settlement have failed is one which is followed and adopted by traditional *durbars* at all levels.[5]

In civil disputes the property, movable or immovable, which is the cause of litigation, is awarded to the side in whose favour a decree is passed. But the *durbar* makes a cut of certain percentage of the total value to reduce its worth so as to discourage people from unwillingness to submit to amicable settlement and also from resorting to litigation. As Rymbai observes, litigation is held as a social evil which is highly disreputable and which should be shunned like ugly sin. It is on account of this that families of litigant parties cut off each other socially completely, especially when the parties are members of the same family or when the parties are the families who belong to the same clan.

In criminal cases corporal punishments of varying degrees are imposed according to the seriousness of the offence extending to dismemberment of limbs or capital sentences for the more heinous crimes. Punishment with indelible tattoo marks is a form of punishment inflicted by clan *durbars* for offences of sex committed by their members between themselves considered as the blackest sacrilege unforgivable before God or man. Minors who happen to get involved in criminal offences are not tried before the *durbars* like adult offenders. Their parents or guardians are admonished to rear them up properly.[6]

In the traditional manner, the practice was that a verbal complaint was made to the *Sordar* or Headman. The facts and circumstances of the case are then detailed before the *Sordar* or Headman. If it was a case in which he and the village elders could adjudicate, then they would summon the parties and fix a date for the hearing of a case. An attempt was always made to effect a compromise between the contending parties. If no reconciliation could be effected, a crier or *u nongpyrta shnong* was sent to announce the whole village to witness the trial of the case. Such announcement having been made, what followed was *ka khang shnong* which means prohibiting the villagers (adult male) from going anywhere but to attend the village *durbar* at the *durbar* ground. Attendance at *durbar* was compulsory. Absence was punishable with fines.

The *durbar* ground was an open space and flat stones served as seats for the *durbaris*. When all have assembled, one of the headmen opened the proceedings, who made a long speech, then other speeches followed. Thereafter, the parties to the dispute threw on the ground in front of the *syiem* a turban, or a bag containing betel, *pan* and lime in front of the *durbar*, as pledges. As already mentioned, attempts at an amicable settlement would be made otherwise evidences produced by the parties or *ki mamla* would be examined and the case would be decided on the strength of the evidence. Deliberations in the form of disputes follow and interpretations are raised. Both the parties were engaged with pleaders known as *riewsaid* who stand as mover for and against the motion. The *durbar* was presided over by the *syiem*, acting as the judge and the whole *durbar* as a jury. Witnesses called *ki sakhi* were also called in to examine the parties.[7]

In former times these witnesses have to take either an oath or a pinch of salt placed on a sword, or a more solemn oath is sworn on *u klong* (a hallow gourd) containing liquor and rice. Traditions state that a session which could not terminate in a day is adjourned till the next morning. If no satisfactory decision could be arrived at the session it may continue for a number of days.[8] At length the finding of the *durbar* is taken, often the *syiem* has summed up, and a sentence is pronounced, which generally consists of a fine in money, almost accompanied by an Order to the losing party to present a pig.[9] This cost of litigation paid by the losing party to the other party which again paid a sort of gratification known as *bainguh* to the court. The aggrieved party might prefer an appeal to the judicial bodies at the higher levels like *Ka Durbar Riad* and *Ka Durbar Syiem*. This used to be the general practice and still followed today. On receipt of an appeal, *Ka Durbar Raid* or *Ka Durbar Syiem* would look into the proceedings followed at the village *durbar* and if they found them satisfactory, the appeal would be dismissed. A sitting fee or *ka bai shylliah* was imposed on both parties.[10]

From the above, it is clear that in the administration of justice, the Khasis observe the due process of law. For the implementation of the decisions of the *durbar* customary laws should be observed. In some cases if all normal systems of trial fail, trials by ordeals are resorted to as a last resort. Yule, quoted by Gurdon, mentioned in his writings in 1844, of the water ordeal called *ka ngam um*. This method was also witnessed by Colonel Maxwell, late Superintendent of the Manipur State in Manipur in 1903. The water ordeal is of two kinds. One such ordeal was *ka ngam ksih* or diver in which the disputants would fix a spear in a deep pool. They would select respective divers or *ki ksih* who would dive and catch hold of the spear. Whoever of the parties remained longest under water without returning to the surface was adjudged by the *Syiem* and the *durbar* to have won the case. Amongst the Khasis sometimes the supporters of the contending parties compelled the divers to remain under water by holding them down with long spears.

Another form of trial was to place two pots in each containing a piece of gold and a piece of silver wrapped up in clothes, in shallow water. The parties were directed to plunge their hands into the water and take up, each of them, one of the pots. The party who brought up a piece of gold was adjudged the victor. If both parties got either gold or silver, then the case was amicably settled by the *durbar*, and if it was a land case, the land was equally divided between the parties.[11] In Khasi Hills, ordeal was resorted only once and that was in Khyrim State during the rulership of Hajon Manik.[12]

The most dreaded ordeal, however, is that of swearing on a gourd of rice beer called *u klong* or *u klong u khnam* where any guilty party is supposed to suffer certain misfortunes like unnatural deaths, or accidents, if the swearing is false. Nobody can force this ordeal on others. One of the parties to the dispute must propose and the opposite party must accept the ordeal, of their own accord and in open court or *durbar*. When the proposal is accepted, a gourd or *u klong* containing fermented rice beer or *ka sohphoh* with an arrow and a barbed iron head planted in the fermented rice is provided. The party desiring to swear in the gourd of rice beer will bring the same to the judge who will invoke the goddess of the State to judge the man. The content of such an invocation brings to the effect that if a person swears falsely, he will surely die. The person who undergoes this type of ordeals wins the case.[13]

The Khasis have got their own laws within the Khasi society which were already in existence. They are as follows:[14] 1) Homicide (*ka pyniap briew*), 2) Murder for the propitiation of *u thlen* (mythical snake) (*ka shohnoh briew*), 3) Adultery (*ka klim*), 4) Rape or molestation (*ka kembor kynthei*), 5) Arson (*ka thang iing*), 6) Black magic or witchcraft (*ka ai ksuid briew*), 7) Robbery or plunder (*ka lute*), 8) Theft (*ka tuh ka thiem*), 9) Incestuous marriage (*ka shongsang*), 10) Marriage between prohibited parties like a marriage between the step-daughter and the step-father (*shong rynri*), 11) False allegations (*tuit bamman*), 12) False complaint (*ka mudui lamler*), 13) Contempt of Durbar (*bein dorbar*), 14) Defamation (*kren ne ka leh be-ijot*), 15) Trespass (*ka kiew iing bor*), 16) Breach of law (*ka ryngkang adong*).

The above crimes were binding when there was (a) quarrel, fighting in the market place or in a main path; (b) cutting trees from *'law kyntang* (religious forest), *'law adong* (reserved forest), *'law lyngdoh* (sacred forest), or spoiling *ki mawbri* (boundary stone), *mawniam* (religious stone) and *maw rukom* (equivalent of sacred stone); (c) to transgress any prohibitions existed by the *durbar*.

Punishment According to Khasi Customary Law

In ancient times, any person who has committed a breach of law is punishable according to the Khasi law. There were also punishments which were inflicted by the *Syiems* and their *durbars* in criminal cases. Punishment may be either reformatory or punitive in character. The first type of punishment is called by the Khasis *pynsuk* and the second is known as *saja*. Reformatory punishment is carried out in the form of imprisonment for a specific period or by the payment of a fine to be paid either in cash or in kind. This type of punishment was awarded in case of theft, cheating or acts intended to inflict physical injury on any person.[15] Capital punishment was awarded for murder or casting of a magic spell on anyone as to make a victim loose his normal senses. The murder was punishable by beating the culprit to death with clubs or *ki tangon-ki-lymban*. Hurling him down a precipice was also another practice.

The punishment of adultery was imprisonment for life or *ka shah dainmur* or a fine of Rs.1,100 and one pig or *ka khadwei spah wei doh*. Punishment for rape was imprisonment for life in the case of the woman being married, and a heavy fine and one pig if the woman was a spinster. Arson was punishable with imprisonment for life, or a heavy fine of Rs.1,100 with one pig. The punishment for causing people to be possessed by devils or *kaba ai ksuid briew* was exile or *ka pynryngkang par* and if the sorcerer's victim died, the sorcerer was hurled down a precipice or *pynnoh khongpong*. The punishment for robbery and theft was the stocks known as *jylla kharit* and *pyndait diengsong* and the imposition of fetter or *pyndait ka nar ka bili*. The practice of *jylla kharit* involves sending a convicted person into exile. Such a person has his head shaven into three patches and riding the bull on the reverse side keeping for him with a provision of meal for the day, at the very sight of which, people at once know that he is an outcaste or excommunicated from the society. The practice of *pyndait diengsong* involves the confinement of a criminal in a cell with his hands and feet tied to wooden poles. There was also a form of punishment known as *kaba syang sohmynken*, in which the culprit was compelled to sit on a bamboo platform under which chillies were burnt, the purpose being to extract confession. The incest or *sang*, which, amongst the Khasis means cohabiting with a member of a man's or woman's own clan, was punishable with exile or a fine of Rs.550/- and one pig. This is regarded by the Khasis as the highest form of taboo, though with a lesser amount of fine. Punishment for damages or *ka mynrain khmat* involves the compensation of Rs.53 and one pig for breach of an agreement assessed by the court against the party who disregards the agreement. Punishment for divorce involves a divorce fee or *ka thnem* paid by either a husband or wife for procuring divorce. However, punishment for deserting the spouse or marry without any ceremony involving a divorce or marriage fine or *ka kaw shiliang ne arliang.*[16]

The punishment for trespass according to Khasi law involves a fine of Rs.106/- and one pig. The punishment for contempt of *durbar* involves a fine or *Dai* which is not more than 4 annas, 8 annas or at the most Re.1/- meted out to persons who ignore the rules of the local *durbar*. The intention of this fine is only to maintain the discipline among the local inhabitants who are expected to respect each other. Further, the punishment for breach of rules of the durbar involves also a fine or *ka dainkuna dainkaid*. The punishment for false allegation etc. involves a fine of Rs.15/- and one pig or *khatsan tyngka wei doh* and punishment for petty crimes involving a small amount of fine of Rs.5/- only and one pig or *san tyngka wei doh.*[17]

From the above, it is seen that according to Khasi law, in case of physical assault, there is no law which really binds a person concerned. If there is any complaint, then they decide in the presence of both the contending parties in dispute. In case, if it is compromised by mutual agreement then a fine is paid by both the parties. Usually, in the case of physical assault, if it is by a small fine then the fine should not be more than Rs.5/- with one pig (*san tyngka wei doh*). But usually, no complaint is lodged against physical assault, because they take it as a friendly tussle only and the dispute is solved by mutual understanding. However, in areas like Sohra, Mawmluh and Mawsmai where physical assault may be caused through bows and arrows and *lathis*, punishment is fixed by the village *durbar*.[18]

In the disposal of cases, the Khasis attach considerable importance to *nia*. Literally the word *nia* implies argument. However, according to the Khasis, the term *nai* has a close relation to *jutang* or understanding. *Nia* alone is not the absolute measure in the administration of justice. Taken together with *jutang*, it constitutes an exhaustive process of utilising to the maximum all the conscience has to speak. In the process of hearing the *nia* given by parties, the *durbar* is supposed to resort to the method of dialectics under which "contradictory ideas are resolved by the process of definition". When *nia* fails to produce *jutang*, the trial is considered as inconclusive and other methods are to be followed.[19]

In matters concerning adjudication of cases, the *Syiem* and his *Myntris* enjoy only residual powers and the lower units of the state like the *raid* and villages have been given wider scope. The courts of the units also have got the power to pass judgements and to pronounce sentences. Such courts have the authority to pass and pronounce capital sentences of which only the *Syiem's durbar* has the power to do so. The *Syiem's durbar* therefore functions as the highest and the final court of appeal.[20]

Notes and References

1. Pakem, B., "Administration of Justice in Jaintia Hills", in S.K.Chattopadhyay (ed.), *The Tribal Institutions of Meghalaya*, Spectrum Publications, Gauhati, 1985, p.173.
2. Costa, G. *Ka Riti Jong ka Ri Laiphew Syiem, Ka Bynta Kaba Ar*, Don Bosco Press, Shillong, 1971, pp.1-2.
3. Gurdon, P.R.T., *The Khasis*, 2nd Edition, Macmillan & Co. Ltd., London, 1914, pp.91-92.
4. Rymbai, R.T., "Relationship Between District Councils, Chief and Village Government – Role of Traditional Institutions", Paper presented in the Seminar on *District Councils and Village Government in North-East India*, under the auspices of IIPA, Shillong Branch and Department of Public Administration, NEHU, Shillong, 23-24 March 1987, p.6.
5. *Ibid.*, p.7.
6. *Ibid.*, p.8.
7. F.n. 3.
8. Bareh, Hamlet, *Khasi Democracy*, Ri Khasi Press, Shillong, 1964, p.65.
9. F.n. 3, pp.92-93.
10. Pdah, S.M. *Khasi Polity with Special Reference to Syiemship*, Unpublished M.Phil Dissertation, 1982.
11. F.n. 3, pp.94-95; F.n. 7, pp.15-17.
12. Kharlukhi, B.R., "Administration of Justice in the Khasi Hills", in S.K. Chattopadhyaya (ed.) *The Tribal Institutions of Meghalaya*, Spectrum Publications, Gauhati, 1985, p.114; F.n. 7, p.8.
13. F.n. 3, pp.95-97.
14. Costa, G. *Ka Jingroi ka Ri Khasi 1: Ka Riti Jong ka Ri*

Laiphew Syiem, St. Anthony's College, Shillong, 1936, pp.162-163.

15. F.n. 12, p.116.
16. F.n. 14, pp.170-171; F.n. 3, pp.93-94.
17. *Ibid.*
18. F.n. 14, p.163.
19. F.n. 12, p.114.
20. *Ibid.*, p.115.

5

ADMINISTRATION OF JUSTICE DURING THE BRITISH RULE

With the coming of the British, certain changes were brought about as the Khasi *Syiems* came under British control by the granting of *sanads*. After the annexation of Khasi Hills by the British in 1833, the Khasi *syiems* were brought under their control and especially when the leader of the *syiems*, Tirot Sing surrendered on 13 January 1833, the rising of the *syiems* subsided. Though the British recognised the *syiem* and his court, but made certain changes in the existing system of administration of justice. The first change was the decision that the *syiem's* courts were appealable. Appeals against the judgement of the *Syiem* were allowed in the court of the Deputy Commissioner appointed by the British. Secondly, the British took away from the *syiems* the right to wage war or enter into any independent treaties, and the right to try cases of murder and culpable homicide. But on the other hand, the British allowed the retention of the traditional offices of the *syiems* and village headmen and these continue to function till today. Yet the fact still remained that the judicial powers of the *Syiem* and the traditional political authorities were curtailed by the British to a limited extent. In Khasi Hills, the British recognised twenty five Khasi States as semi-independent and dependent States. Cherra, Khyrim, Nongstoin, Langrin and Nongspung were referred to as semi-independent States as they had never been actually coerced by a British force. The remaining twenty States recognised as dependent States were those that had been restored to their *syiems* or in the case of the five *Sirdarships* were those States that were created by the British.[1]

The *syiems* of the semi-independent States were permitted to exercise, with the help of the *durbars* and elders, sole criminal and civil jurisdiction in their respective States over their own subjects on matters pertaining exclusively to them. The dependent *syiems* were permitted to investigate and decide all civil and criminal cases in which the parties with their own people, with the exception of cases of murder, homicide and accidental deaths which were reported to the Cherra authorities for their decision.[2] Both categories of States were bound to take to the Cherra Court cases in which British subjects and the inhabitants of more than one State were concerned.[3]

By Act 1835, the Political Agent was placed incharge of civil and criminal cases in the Khasi Hills under the Superintendent of Suddar *Dewani* (Civil) and *Nazamut Adalat* (criminal) respectively. The Junior Assistant Commissioner was appointed as Administrator of Jaintia Hills and a British portion of Khasi States. Before this arrangement was made the system of administration of justice which was started in 1833 was continued upto 1841. After 1841, the *syiem* heard all civil cases upto a certain limit and all criminal cases not of a heinous character in which the people of their own village were concerned. This state of affair continued until 1869, when the Garo Hills

Act (Act XXII) of 1869, was applied to Khasi Hills on 1 November 1871.[4]

By a promulgation issued under the Government of India Act, 1870, on 6 February 1874, Assam was made a separate administration under the Chief Commissioner and its territories included among others Khasi and Jaintia Hills. After its constitution as a Chief Commissioner's province, it was a Scheduled District under the Scheduled District Act (Act XIV of 1874). Under this Act, the administration of criminal justice in the Khasi and Jaintia Hills was vested on the Commissioner of Assam, the Deputy Commissioner and his assistants and the recognised village authorities such as the *Syiems*, *Wahadadars*, *Sirdars* and *Lyngdohs* authorised by the head of the province.

The Deputy Commissioner was competent to pass a sentence of death transportation or imprisonment up to the maximum amount provided for the offence, provided that the death sentence or sentences of imprisonment of seven years shall be subject to the confirmation of the Chief Commissioner. The Deputy Commissioner authorised the village elders to dispose of minor cases and inflict fines up to Rs.50.[5]

After the British Parliament passed the Government of India Act, 1935, another Order in Council was issued, namely, the Indian (Foreign Jurisdiction) Order in Council, 1937, amending the Indian (Foreign Jurisdiction) Order in Council, 1902. According to this Act, the 'King' (His Majesty) with the advice of his Privy Council to Order, which met on 18 March 1937, states that as from the commencement of the Government of India Act, 1935, the powers conferred by the Principal Order on the Governor General in Council shall be powers of His Majesty's Representative for the exercise of these functions of the

Crown, and he may obligate those powers to such extent and in such manner as he thinks fit.[6]

According to the Government of India Act, 1935, India as on 1 April 1937, was a very big country. It comprised of "British India", "Indian States" and "Tribal Areas" in accordance with Section 311 of the Government of India Act, 1935, passed by the British Parliament in 1935. Generally speaking, administration of British India was carried on by and through the Governor-General and that of "Indian States" by and through the Crown Representative. But the same person, with a title of "Viceroy", was appointed the Governor-General and the Crown Representative. In matters relating to and connected with the "Tribal Areas" the Governor-General in Council is pleased to direct the Governor of Assam to discharge his functions as his agent. Beyond the external boundaries of the Province of Assam, all functions hitherto discharged and in relation to the tribal areas, the Governor of Assam was to act as Agent to the Governor-General in respect of the political control of the trans-border tribes, the administration of the tribal areas and the administration of the Assam Rifles and other Armed Civil Forces.[7]

In so far as the administration of justice in the Khasi and Jaintia Hills District is concerned, the administration of justice was governed by the Rules for the Administration of Justice and Police in the Khasi and Jaintia Hills prescribed by the Governor in exercise of the powers vested in him by Section Six(6) of the Scheduled Districts Act, 1874 (Act XIV of 1874) issued under Notification No.2618-A.P., dated 29 March 1937 cancelling all previous Orders on the subjects. The rules of their own force extend to the whole of the Khasi and Jaintia Hills District but did not apply to the "Khasi States", substantial portions thereof were extended to those States by the Crown Representative, acting under the Indian (Foreign Jurisdiction) Order in Council issued under Notification No.164-IB, dated 18 August 1937, of the Foreign Jurisdiction Act.[8] Incidentally, the Rules *per se* did not confer any judicial power on any village authorities unless the Deputy Commissioner conferred the power on him and recognised it by the grant of a *Sanad.*[9] The rules, however, were issued by virtue of the powers vested in the Governor of Assam by the Schedule District Act, 1974.

Under Section 2 of the above mentioned Rules, 1937 the Police of the Khasi and Jaintia Hills shall consist of (a) Regular Police subject to Act of 1861; and (b) Rural Police, consisting of *Sardars, Dolois, Pators, Lyngdohs* and other village authorities recognised by the Deputy Commissioner. The control of the rural police in the Khasi and Jaintia Hills as per Section 3 of the Rules is vested in the Deputy Commissioner acting under the Orders of the Governor. Misconduct on the part of the rural police is punishable by fine amounting to Rs.500/- or by punishment awarded under the penal code for a like offence. Only the Deputy Commissioner or other officers may be awarded for imprisonment. Section 4 states that Rural Police shall not be deemed to be Police Officers for the purposes of Section 25 and 26 of the Indian Evidence Act or Section 162 of the Criminal Procedure Code. Section 5 states that an appeal from Sardars, *Dolois* and other chief village authorities in police matters lies with the Deputy Commissioner, whose Orders are final.[10]

With regards to Regular Police, Section 6 states that Regular Police form part of the general police force of the provinces under the control of the Inspector General of Police, Assam, and are subject to the ordinary rules of police, modified by the Governor or the Inspector General of Police from time to time. The function of the Regular Police as per Section 7 shall act only when required by general or on special order of the Governor, Deputy Commissioner, or other officer duly authorised to the force any portion of the duties of police in any locality. The ordinary duties of police shall be discharge under Section 8 by the *Sardars* and *Dolois* and other village authorities duly authorised by the Deputy Commissioner. These police shall arrest all criminals within their respective jurisdiction. Section 9 further states that it is the duty of the *Sardars, Dolois,* and other chief village authorities to report to the Deputy Commissioner all crimes, violent deaths, on serious accidents occurring in their districts, and all occurrences within or beyond their jurisdiction, likely to affect the public peace from the place of arrest to the court of such officer.[11]

The duties of *Sardars, Dolois* and other village authorities under Section 10 shall watch and report and in every emergent case may apprehend if found in their jurisdictions within a period of twenty-four hours of arrest from the place of arrest to the court of an officer authorised to take cognisance.

On the occurrence of any heinous crime[12] Section 4 states that any village officer by custom or appointment, shall at once apprehend the offender, and in any case report to the *Sardar* or *Doloi*, or other chief village authority, if the offender has not been apprehended proceed to the place where the crime occurred and enquire into the matter. If a crime has been committed he will immediately report it to the Deputy Commissioner, whether the offender has been apprehended or not. Section 12 states that the jurisdiction of the *Sardars, Dolois* and other village authorities may pursue beyond their jurisdiction. Ordinarily, no *Sardar, Doloi* or village authority shall attempt to arrest an offender beyond his own jurisdiction without the cognisance and co-operation of the *Sardar*, *Doloi* or chief village authority of the village to which the offender has fled. When the *Sardars*, *Dolois*, or other chief village authorities feel unable to arrest an offender, Section 13 states that they must apply to the Deputy Commissioner, or any officer duly authorised to grant them such aid. Further, Section 14 empowered the *Sardars*, *Dolois* and other chief village authorities to arrest and also fine, all drunkards and other disorderly persons found brawling and of their houses, and all person found gambling.[13] Further, Section 15 states that all the inhabitants of the Khasi and Jaintia Hills are bound to aid the regular police and village authorities in the maintenance of Order, or the apprehension of offenders. Any person failing to do so is liable to fine. Further, when the particular persons blameable for failure to aid in any community cannot be ascertained, the *Sardar*, *Doloi* or chief village authority shall be considered responsible. However, if it appears that the community is to blame and the offenders cannot be discovered, a fine may be imposed upon the community by the Deputy Commissioner.[14]

In so far as the administration of criminal justice is concerned, Section 16 of the Rules, 1937, states that criminal justice shall be administered by the Deputy Commissioner, his Assistants, and by the *Sardars*, *Dolois* and other chief village authorities. Section 16(1) further states that an Assistant to the Deputy Commissioner is competent to try an offence under Section 147 of the Indian Penal Code relating to punishment for rioting even if both the parties belong to Khasi tribe. Section 17 also states that the Deputy Commissioner was competent to pass a sentence of death, transportation or imprisonment up to the maximum amount provided for the offence and a fine up to any amount provided that all sentences of death, transportation or imprisonment of seven years and upwards shall be subject to the confirmation by the High Court of Assam. Further, the High Court or Deputy Commissioner may call for the proceedings of any officer subordinate to him, but no offence shall be perished by a sentence exceeding under the Indian penal code. However, Assistants to the Deputy Commissioner shall exercise such powers, not exceeding those of a magistrate of the First Class as define in the Criminal Procedure Code. Further, Section 17(A) states that when the Deputy Commissioner passes sentence of death, the proceedings shall be submitted to the High Court and the sentence shall not be executed unless it was confirmed by the High Court. Also Section 17(B) states that the Deputy Commissioner shall inform the accused of the period (2 days) within which, if the accused wishes to appeal, his appeal should be preferred. Section 17(c) states that under Rule 17(A) the High Court (a) may confirm the sentence or pass any other sentence warranted by law, or (b) may annul the conviction and convict the accused of any offence of which the Deputy Commissioner might have convicted the accused, or order a new trial on the same, or an amended charge, or (c) may acquit the accused person provided that no order of confirmation shall be made until the period allowed for preferring an appeal has expired. If an appeal is presented within such period, until such appeal is disposed of. Further Section 17(d) states that when a sentence of death passed by the Deputy Commissioner was submitted to the High Court for confirmation, on receiving the order of confirmation or other order of the High Court, the Deputy Commissioner shall, cause such order to be carried into effect by issuing a warrant in the form given in Schedule V, No.XXXV of the Criminal Procedure Code. Section 17(E) empowered the Deputy Commissioner to fix the time and place of execution, which shall not be less than 21 or more than 28 days from the date of issue of warrant.[15]

In matters relating to the disposal of petty cases, Section 18 of the Rules, 1937, states that the Deputy Commissioner may empower any *Sardar* or any village authority to dispose of cases relating to offences involving damage to property not exceeding Rs.50/- injury to person not affecting life or limb, house-trespass and theft where the value of property did not exceed Rs.50/-. In such cases, these village authorities are competent to impose a fine for any offence triable by them, up to the amount of Rs.50/-. They may also award restitution or compensation to the extent of the injury sustained, and enforce it by attaching the property of the offenders. In cases in which the fine is not paid or realised, they shall represent the facts and send in the offender to the Deputy Commissioner, who may retry the case and impose such other punishment, as he is competent to inflict. Each *Sardar*, *Doloi*, or other chief village authority who may be empowered as mentioned above, shall receive a *sanad* of recognition under the signature of the Deputy Commissioner.[16]

As regards the power of village authorities to decide and carry out decision, Section 19 of the Rules, 1937, empower the *Sardars*, *Doloi* or other village authorities to carry out their decision, or order attachment of property as soon as judgement is pronounced. But in no case if property so attached to be sold if the convicted party claim to appeal within eight days, without the orders of the Deputy Commissioner. Further, *Sardars*, *Dolois* or recognised village authorities cannot decide in cases (a) where the defendant is not a native of the Khasi and Jaintia Hills or not the resident within their jurisdiction; or (b) when the offence is against the state, or has caused death or danger of life, or amounts to robbery or concerns counterfeiting of coin, or making of fraudulent documents. As regard the procedure to decide by the village authorities, Section 20 states that the *Sardars, Dolois* or recognised village authorities shall decide all cases in open *Dorbar*, in the presence of at least three witnesses and the complainant and accused, whose attendance are empowered to compel. The party may appeal to the Deputy Commissioner or. his Assistant within 16 days of the decision. Section 21 states that an appeal from the decision of an Assistant to the Deputy Commissioner within thirty days of the order appealed against, excluding the time required for procuring a copy of the order. Section 22 states that an appeal lie to the High Court from any sentence passed by the Deputy Commissioner or Additional Deputy Commissioner within thirty days of the date of the order appealed against, excluding the time required for procuring a copy of the order. In case of a death sentence, the appeal must be preferred within seven days.[17] Also Section 22A states that the Governor may direct such an appeal to be presented to the High Court from an original or appellate court passed by any court other than the high court within ninety days from the date of the order excluding the time needed for obtaining a copy of the order. The procedure of the High Court, the Deputy Commissioner and his Assistant as per Section 23 shall be in the spirit of the code of criminal procedure as far as it is applicable to the circumstances of the district and consistent with these rules.[18] The chief exceptions are:[19]

a) Only verbal order or notice of summon, etc., shall be requisite, except when the regular police are employed, or the person concerned is not resident in the district at the time, or if in the district but resident beyond it. But verbal order shall be for a fixed day, not exceeding sixteen days from which the order is issued, and be made known to the person affected, or to some adult member of his family to allow him to appear.

b) The form prescribed by Section 263 of the code of Criminal Procedure Code may be used for all cases specified in Section 260 by all officers with first class powers. Examinations and proceedings shall generally be recorded in English only.

c) The proceedings of *Sardars*, *Dolois*, or other recognised village authorities, need not be in writing. But if before trial the village authorities can find any person who can write, a brief note of the proceedings is to be made.

d) All the fine levied by the *Sardars*, *Dolois* or other recognised village authorities shall be paid to the Deputy Commissioner or Assistant Commissioner or other officers empowered, within eight days from the date of realization. The Deputy Commissioner is authorised to pay small stipends to those village authorities that give him satisfaction provided the total amount should not exceed the sum of the fines realised by all the village authorities during the year.

e) It shall be discretionary to examine witness on oath in any form, or to warn them that they are liable to punishment for perjury if they state that they knew to be false.

With regard to an inquiry commission, Section 23A of the Rules, 1937, states that in the course of an inquiry, trial or other proceedings, it appears to the High Court or the Court of the Deputy Commissioner that the examination of a witness is necessary for the ends of justice, and that the attendance of such witnesses cannot be procured. Under the circumstances of the case, such court may issue a commission for the examination of the witness following the spirit of the code of criminal procedure, 1898. Also, Section 23B states that whenever a commission for the examination of witness issued under any law for the time being in force is received by the Deputy Commissioner, he or such of his Assistant having the power of a Magistrate of the First Class appoint on this behalf, shall execute and return the Commission following the spirit of the Code of Criminal Procedure, 1898. Further, Section 24B empowered the President or the Governor on conditions or without conditions to suspend the execution of any sentence or remit any punishment. If any sentence has been suspended or remitted, the President or the Governor may cancel the remission and order the sentence to be carried out, and the person in whose favour the sentence had been suspended or remitted, may be arrested by the police officer without warrant and remanded to undergo the unexpired portion of the sentence.[20]

In so far as the administration of civil justice in the Khasi and Jaintia Hills district is concerned, Section 25 of the Rules, 1937, states that the administration is entrusted to the Deputy Commissioner, his Assistants, *Sardars* and *Dolois* and other chief village authorities. In cases which may be tried by village authorities, Section 26 states that the *Sardars*, *Dolois* and other chief village authorities may be recognised by the Deputy Commissioner by *sanad* under his signature as competent to try cases without limit, but with the following reservations: (a) they may not try suits in which their fathers, mothers, sons, daughters, uncles, aunts, sisters, brothers, the children or any near relatives are parties, nor bring a suit in which a native of the plains, or native of another *Sardarship* not resident in their jurisdiction are parties; (b) all suits must be decided in open *Dorbar* in the presence of the parties and at least three respectable witnesses.[21] It was held with reference to this provision in the Rules of 1937, that the trial of a suit by the *Dorbars* was not vitiated simply because the plaintiff is one of the *dorbaris.*[22]

Further Section 27 empower the *Sardars* and other recognised village authorities to compel attendance of parties to any suit, being residents within their own jurisdiction, and to fine within the limit of Rs.50/-. Section 28 also states that all proceedings shall be viva voce and the *sardars* or other recognised village authorities shall not be called upon to make record of their decision. But if at the trial before the village authorities, can find any person who can write, a brief note of the proceedings is to be made. Section 29, further states that the *sardars* or other village authorities may carry out their decision at once, but in no case if the party claims to appeal within thirty days. Section 30 states that the procedure for notices given by *sardars* and other village authorities to parties or witnesses may be verbal, and for a fixed day not exceeding eight days from the day it is given. Section 31 further states that the Deputy Commissioner and his Assistants shall not ordinarily hear suits triable by *sardars* and other village authorities, but they have a discretion to do so when suits, which the village authorities cannot try, must be tried by the Deputy Commissioner or his Assistants. Section 33 also states that an appeal shall lie from the decision of the *sardar* or other recognised village authority to the Deputy Commissioner, or an Assistant to the Deputy Commissioner. Section 34 states that properties, movable or immovable; belonging to the judgement-debtor is liable to attachment and sale in execution or decree. Further, Section 35 states that there shall be no imprisonment for debt, excepting in cases where the Deputy Commissioner is satisfied that fraudulent disposal of property has taken place; in such cases the debtor may be detained for a period not exceeding six months.[23]

Under Section 36A the High Court or Deputy Commissioner may on application or otherwise call for the proceedings of any case decided by any subordinate officer and passed such orders as he may deem fit. The Deputy Commissioner shall be a court of appeal from a decision of an Assistant. The High Court shall be a court of appeal from an original decision of the Deputy Commissioner. The decree of the appellate court shall be transferred to the court passing the original Order for execution as decree of its own. Further, Section 36B states that if the appeal fails the money deposited or received shall immediately be paid to the respondent. Section 37 states that the High Court and the Courts of the Deputy Commissioner or the Additional Deputy Commissioner and his Assistants shall be guided by the spirit, but not bound by the letter, of the Code of Civil Procedure.[24] As regard administration of justice in Khasi States during the British rule the administration was administered in accordance with the provisions contaned in the "*sanads*" issued to the "Heads" (*Syiem*, *Lyngdoh*, *Wahadadar* and *Sardar Hima*) of the Khasi States.

Notes and References

1. Allen, W.J., *Report on the Administration of the Cossyah and Jynteah Hill Territory*, 1858, Shillong, reprint. 1903, p.28; Gurdon, P.R.T., *The Khasis*, Cosmo Publications, Delhi, reprint. 1975, p.75.
2. By Cherra authorities we mean the Political Agency which was created on 11 February, 1835.
3. F.n. 1, pp.26-28.
4. Mills, A.J.M., *Report on the Khasi and Jaintia Hills*, Calcutta, 1853, Reprint. 1985, NEHU Publications, Shillong, 1985, pp.119-120.
5. Rao, V.V. *et al.*, *A Century of Government and Politics in North East India*, Vol.I, Assam (1874-1980), S. Chand & Co., New Delhi, 1983, pp.215-216.
6. "The Indian (Foreign Jurisdiction) Order, 1937:, in *The Sixth Schedule to the Constitution of India: A Study*, by Hansaria, B.L. (Smt. Gita Hansaria, Kharghuli, Gauhati, 1983), pp.A.295-296.
7. Shullai, L.G., *Ka Extra Provincial Jurisdiction Act, 1947, bad Kiwei De Ki Ain Hapoh ka Bri U Hynñiewtrep, Series I* (n.d.), Unpublished, pp.1-2.
8. Sangma, Jangsan, *Law of Administration of Justice in Meghalaya* (Jansan Sangma, Tura, 1973), pp.1-2.
9. Indian Law Institute, New Delhi, *Customary Law and Justice in the Tribal Areas of Meghalaya*, prepared by Kusum & Bakshi, P.M. (11.M, Tripathi, Bombay, 1982), pp.20-27.
10. Rules for the Administration of Justice and Police in the Khasi and Jaintia Hills, 1937, in Sangma, Jangsan, *Law of Administration of Justice in Meghalaya*, (Jansan Sangma, Tura, 1937), pp.2-3.
11. *Ibid.*, p.4.
12. Heinous crimes – include rebellion, riots, counterfeiting coin or passing counterfeit coin, murder, wounding to the injury of life or limbs, rape, robbery, dacoity, castle-stealing, arson, house-breaking, forgery.

13. F.n. 10, pp.5-6.
14. *Ibid.*, p.6.
15. *Ibid.*, pp.7-10.
16. *Ibid.*, p.10.
17. *Ibid.*, pp.11-12.
18. *Ibid.*, p.12.
19. *Ibid.*, pp.12-13.
20. *Ibid.*, pp.15-17.
21. *Ibid.*, p.19.
22. "Ka Syndur Lakiang V. U Kistobin Rymbai, I.U.C. (Assam) 66 (1948-1953)" cited F.n. 8, p.169.
23. *Ibid.*, pp.19-24.
24. *Ibid.*, pp.24-27.

6

ADMINISTRATION OF JUSTICE DURING AND AFTER INDEPENDENCE

With the advent of Independence, the twenty-five Khasi States, that is, *Syiemship*, *Lyngdohship*, *Sirdarship* and *Wahadadarship* had formed themselves into a federation of Khasi States in 1946. The *Dorbar* of the Federation of Khasi States which included all the Khasi States as members agrees that with effect from 15 August 1947, all existing administrative arrangements between the province of Assam and the Indian Union and the Khasi States shall, with the exception to be noted below, continue in force for a period of two years or until new or modified arrangements have been arrived at between the respective authorities concerned. The Federation signed the Instrument of Accession of the Khasi Hills States which was accepted by the then Governor-General of India on 17 August 1948. In the Annexed agreement to the Instrument of Accession, the Khasi States agreed with the exceptions that for judicial matters (a) the Federation will set up a competent court of the Federation to exercise the judicial functions formerly vested in the Political Officer; (b) in matter of customary laws there will be no appeal from the Court of the Federation. In other cases, an appeal will lie to the Governor until a High Court of Assam was established when such appeal will lie to the Assam High Court; (c) the judicial authority exercised by State Courts in respect of Khasis would be maintained; (d) in regard to all non-Khasis the judicial arrangement as existed would continue for the present except that the Judicial Powers of the Political Officer would be vested in the Court of the Federation when its competence was recognised. Where non-Khasis had voluntarily agreed to submit to the jurisdiction of a State Court that Court would continue to be the original trying Court. Where State Courts comply with certain conditions to be laid down they may be vested with First, Second or Third Class Powers as defined in the Criminal Procedure Court and their jurisdiction would include both Khasi and non-Khasis. The Chief Justice of the Assam High Court, when established, would assume this power which was vested in the Governor.[1]

An exception had been made in the case of Shillong Administered areas covering the Shillong Municipality and Cantonment. It appears from the Government of India, Ministry of States Notification No.166-I.B. dated 16 March 1948, that the rules relating to Civil Justice as contained in Section IV of the Rules, 1937, in so far as all courts, including the High Court of Assam was applicable and subject to any amendments to which they are for the same time being subject in other areas of the State of Assam, shall apply to the Shillong Administered Areas.[2]

Certain changes also took place such as the application of the Indian Penal Code and Rules relating to civil and criminal justice under the Scheduled District Act, 1974, and published with Notification No.2618-A.P., dated 29 March 1937, to the Khasi States vide Central Government

Order No.165-I.B., dated 16 March 1948, made under Extra Provincial Jurisdiction Act, 1947, published in the Assam Gazette dated 29 March 1948. The Order of 16 March 1948, was however, superseded and was issued by another Order known as the Khasi States Federation (Administration of Justice) Orders, 1948, made by the Government of India under Extra-Provincial Jurisdiction Act, 1947, published under Notification No.237-P dated New Delhi, the 16 June 1948. This Order extends to the whole of the Khasi States Federation excluding the Shillong Administered Areas.[3]

Under the Khasi States Federation (Administration of Justice) Order, 1948, relating to criminal justice, Section 2 states that it shall be administered by the Court of the Federation, its Subordinate Courts and the State Courts; Section 3 also states that the Indian Penal code shall apply to the Khasi States Federation as it applies to the Province of Assam; Section 4(i) further states that the Court of the Federation shall be competent to pass sentences of death, transportation or imprisonment up to the maximum amount provided for the offence, and of fine up to any amount; Section 4(2) provided that all sentences of death or transportation shall be subject to the confirmation of the High Court of Assam; Section 4(3) also states that the High Court may call for the proceedings of the Court of the Federation or any of its Subordinate Courts or any of the State Courts or remand the case for retrial; Section 5 further provides that when the Court of the Federation passes sentence of death the proceedings shall be submitted to the High Court of Assam; Section 6 also states that the Court of the Federation shall inform the accused of the period (namely 7 days), if he wishes to appeal; Section 7 also provides that when a sentence of death passed by the Court of the Federation is submitted to the

High Court of Assam for confirmation, the court of the Federation shall, on receiving the order, cause such order by issuing a warrant in form No.XXXV of Schedule V to the Code of Criminal Procedure, 1898; Section 8 further states that the Court of the Federation shall fix the time and place of execution; the time fixed shall not be less han 21 or more than 28 days from the date of issue of the warrant.[4]

Section 9 of the order, 1948, further states that an appeal shall lie from the decision of the Subordinate Court to the Court of the Federation preferred within 30 days, provided that no appeal shall lie against the sentences of fine only passed by a Magistrate of the First Class, when the amount of fine does not exceed Rs.50/-. Section 10 also states that no appeal shall lie from any sentence passed by the Court of Federation involving less than three years imprisonment. Section 11 further provides that the procedure of the High Court of Assam, the Court of the Federation and its Subordinate Courts shall be in the spirit of the code of criminal procedure, 1898, as far as it is applicable in the Khasi States; Section 12 states that a Pleader or *Mukhtar* who is entitled to practice in the High Court of the Dominion of India, and in the District Court of Shillong may appear in any case with the permission in the Court of the Federation and its Subordinate Courts; also Section 13 states that the registers (i) Register of petitions; (ii) Register of crimes; (iii) Register of criminal cases disposed of and (iv) Register of fines be kept in the Court of the Federation.[5]

With regard to civil justice, Section 14 states that the administration is entrusted to the Court of the Federation, its Subordinate and the State Courts; Section 15(1) further states that a State Court can adjudicate any civil cases arising within the State; Sub-Section (2) also states that in regard to non-Khasis and non-State Khasis the Subordinate Courts of the Federation will be the Court of first instance; Section 17, however, states that the Court of the Federation and its Subordinate Courts shall, in all cases in which the parties are indigenous inhabitants of the hills, endeavour to induce them to submit their case to the traditional court; Section 18 states that an appeal shall lie from the decision of the Subordinate Courts and the State Courts to the Court of the Federation.

In all civil matters the Court of the Federation will adjudicate according to the personal laws of the parties and the spirit of the Civil Procedure Code will be followed without prejudice to the local customs and usages.[6] Further, Section 19 provides that moveable or immovable, belonging to the judgement debtor, is liable to attachment and sale in execution of a decree; Section 20 also states that there shall be no imprisonment for debt, except in cases where the Court of the Federation is satisfied that fraudulent disposal has taken place, in such cases the debtor may be detained for a period not exceeding six months; Section 24 also states that the Court of the Federation and its Subordinate Courts shall be guided by the spirit, but not bound by the letter, of the code of Civil Procedure, 1908; Section 25 Sub-Section (1) and (2) states that a Pleader or *Mukhtar* who is entitled to practice in the High Court of the Dominion of India and in the District Court of Shillong may also practice in the Courts of the Federation with the permission of the Federation; Section 27 further provides that the registers: (i) Registers of petitions; (ii) Register of suits tried; and (iii) Register of execution cases be kept by the Court of Federation.[7]

Subsequently, in October 1948, the Government of India issued another Order known as the Khasi States Federation (Administration of Justice) (Supplemental)

Order, 1948, which was published publicly in the Notification No.296-P, dated 4 October 1948, of the Government of India, Ministry of States. The order came into force from 1 July 1948, in the Notification published in the Gazette No.1 July 1/1948 of the Federation of Khasi States issued by the Adviser to the Government of Assam for Excluded Areas and States.[8]

This order extends to the territories to which the Khasi States Federation (Administration of Justice) Order, 1948 extends. Section 3(a) of the (Administration of Justice) (Supplemental) Order, 1948 states that the Agent of the Dominion of India in Khasi States shall be competent to exercise throughout the Federation Criminal Jurisdiction which vested in the Court of Federation under the (Administration of Justice) Order, 1948; (b) the assistants of the Agent, as may be authorised by the Agent of the Dominion of India, shall be competent to exercise throughout the Federation such criminal jurisdiction vested with by the Agent. Section 4(a) also states that an appeal made by the Agent of the Dominion of India in Khasi States, shall lie to the High Court of Assam and (b) where the order is made by any of the Assistants to the Agent. Further, Section 5 states that the provision of Clause 3, Sub-Clause (1) and (3) of Clause 4 and Clauses 5 to 13 of the Khasi States Federation (Administration of Justice) Order, 1948 relating to criminal justice, shall so far as they may be applicable, apply to this order if (i) the Agent was a Court of Federation and the Assistants of the Agent authorised by him under Clause 3 of this order were the Subordinate Courts of the Federation; and (ii) provided that no appeal shall lie against a sentence of fine only passed by an assistant of the agent, when the amount of fine does not exceed Rs.500/-.[9] The Court of the Federation of Khasi States was competent to pass sentences of death, transportation or imprisonment upto the maximum amount provided for the offence. The Court adjudicated according to the personal laws of the parties concerned and the spirit of the Civil Procedure Code in civil matters and of the Criminal Procedure Code in criminal matters. The Court function for two-and-a-half years. No appeal from the decisions in matters of customary laws was made.[10]

Further, in pursuance of Paragraph 4(2) of the Khasi States Federation (Administration of Justice) Order, 1948, issued by the Government of India, Ministry of States, in their Notification No.237-P, dated the 16th June 1948, the Federation of Khasi States with the approval of the High Court of Judicature in Assam, was further enhanced by investing more judicial powers on Mr. A.S. Khongphai as a Second Judicial Officer, Court of the Federation of Khasi States[11] with powers of a Magistrate of First Class and powers under Sections 30, 108, 110, 143, 144, 186, 260, 407, 524 of the Criminal Procedure Code and power to try cases under Section 124A of the Indian Penal Code. The above powers are in addition to the powers already invested on Mr. Khongphai according to Notification No.KSE/2/Jud, dated the 29th July 1948.

In 1949, in exercise of the powers conferred by Section 4 of the Extra Provincial Jurisdiction Act, 1947 (Act No.XLVII of 1947), as delegated to the Governor of Assam by the Government of India, Ministry of States Notification No.335-I.B., dated 3rd November 1948, and of all other powers enabling the Governor of Assam in this behalf, and in supersession of all previous orders on the subject existing prior to the 15 August 1947, the Governor of Assam made the Khasi States (Application of Laws) Order, 1949 issued under Notification No.SK.40/48/83 dated 1st June 1949 published in the Gazette of Assam, Part II, 8th

June 1949. According to Section 6 of this order, 1949, any Court or Authority may construe the provision of any enactment applied by this order thereunder with such modifications not effecting the substance as may be necessary in order to adapt them to the matter before the Court or Authority; the order further provided that any order passed, in any case or in relation to the Khasi States, Shillong Administered Areas, with effect from 15 August 1947, by any Officer or Authority on whom powers are conferred shall be deemed to have been passed and the order shall apply accordingly.[12]

Notes and References

1. Basan, LL.D., *The Khasi States under the Indian Union (Ki Hima Khasi Hapoh Ka India Union)*, (LL.D. Basan, Shillong, dated 2 December 1948), pp.6-7.
2. Sangma, Jangsan, *Law of Administration of Justice in Meghalaya* (Jangsan Sangma, Tura, 1973), p.48.
3. Government of India, Ministry of States, *Notification No.1, July 1, 1948*, p.1.
4. *Ibid.*, pp.1-2.
5. *Ibid.*, p.2.
6. *Ibid.*
7. *Ibid.*, pp.3-4.
8. Shullai, L.G., *Ki Hima Khasi* (L.G. Shullai, Shillong, 1974), p.4.
9. Shullai, L.G., Seminar Paper on "Administration of Justice in Meghalaya" organised by the Law Research Institute, Eastern Region, Guwahati High Court on 4th September, 1999 at State Central Library, Shillong, Appendix 'B'.
10. F.n. 8, pp.47-48.
11. *Notification No.KSF/3/JUD, dated 15th September, 1948*, published in the Gazette of the Federation of Khasi States (No.4, Shillong, December 8, 1948).

12. Assam Gazette, *The Khasi Syiemships (Application of Laws) Order, 1949* (As adopted and modified by the Assam Autonomous Districts (Administration of Justice) Regulation, 1952), Notification No.SK/40/48/83 dated 1st June 1949, p.1.

7

ADMINISTRATION OF JUSTICE IN THE DISTRICT COUNCIL

The Khasi States were brought within the boundary of an Autonomous District known as United Khasi-Jaintia Hills Autonomous District vide Sub-Paragraph (1) of Paragraph 20 of the Sixth Schedule to the Constitution of India as originally adopted on 26 November 1949. The Court of the Federation of Khasi States ceased to function with effect from 26 January 1950, as the Khasi States (Administration of Justice) Order, 1948, issued by the Government of India, Ministry of States Notification No.237-P, dated 16 June 1948, and the Khasi States (Administration of Justice) (Supplemental) Order, 1948, issued by the Government of India, Ministry of States, Notification No.296-P, dated 4 October 1948, were cancelled. This appears in Paragraph 36 of the Khasi States (Administration of Justice) Order, 1950, issued by the Governor of Assam in the Notification No.SK/140/49/8 dated 25 January 1950.[1]

When the Constitution came into force, the Rules for the Administration of Justice, 1937, made on 29 March 1937, were in force in the area within the Municipality of

Shillong, and forming part of the State of Mylliem. The lapse of paramountcy of British Crown and the creation of new relationship under the Instrument of Accession and the agreement which formed part of the Instrument of Accession did not in anyway affect the applicability of the Rules for the administration of Civil Justice so far as the Shillong Administered area was concerned. When a person derives his right from the State and exercising judicial power vested in a State, he functions as a Court. The Assistant to the Deputy Commissioner, when dealing with matters under the Indian Succession Act, is a civil court.[2]

On 25 January 1950, the Governor of Assam in exercise of the powers conferred by Section 4 of the Extra Provincial Jurisdiction Act, 1947, (XLVII of 1947), as delegated to the Governor by the Government of India in the Ministry of States by their Notification No.335-I.B. dated the 3rd November 1948, and of all other powers enabling him in this behalf, the Governor of Assam issued another Order known as the Khasi States (Administration of Justice) Order, 1950, under Notification No.S.K./140/49/8 dated 25 January 1950.[3]

According to Section 1(2) of the Khasi States (Administration of Justice) Order, 1950, applied to the areas of the United Khasi-Jaintia Hills District which were known as Khasi States immediately before the commencement of the Constitution of India, excluding so much of the district as is comprised in the Municipality of Shillong. On the criminal side, Section 2 of the Order states that criminal justice was administered by the Deputy Commissioner or Additional Deputy Commissioner, Khasi and Jaintia Hills District and his Assistants and also by the *Syiems*, *Sirdars*, *Lyngdohs* or *Wahadadars*. Section 4(1) empowers the Deputy Commissioner or Additional Deputy Commissioner to pass any sentence authorised under the Indian Penal Code or any other law for the time being in force in the Khasi States; but any sentence of death or transportation shall be subject to the confirmation by the High Court of Assam. Section 4(2) states that the Courts of the Assistants to the Deputy Commissioner and of the *Syiem* of the Khasi States, shall exercise such powers, not exceeding those of a Magistrate of the First Class as defined in the Code of Criminal Procedure, 1898, as they may be invested with the Governor of Assam.

An appeal shall lie to the Deputy Commissioner or Additional Deputy Commissioner from the Assistant to the Deputy Commissioner preferred within thirty and sixty days respectively of the date of the order. Any person convicted on a trial by the Deputy Commissioner may appeal to the High Courts. Such appeal must be presented within thirty days from the date of the order appealed against.[4]

The (Administration of Justice) Order, 1950, also provides special provision to the Court of a *Syiem* of a State. Section 16 states that the *Syiems*' Courts which were established under the customary law of the state recognised as such by the Governor of Assam, could try any offences under the Indian Penal Code or under any other law for the time being in force within its respective locality except those punishable with death, transportation or involving a punishment of five years which may arise within the limits of its locality and in which the Khasis who reside or hold land within its locality are concerned. Provided, that the *Syiem's* Court could exercise jurisdiction over non-Khasis only if the parties voluntarily invoke or submit to its jurisdiction.[5]

With regard to Civil Justice, Section 18 entrusted to the Deputy Commissioner, Additional Deputy Commissioner, Assistants to the Deputy Commissioner and Courts of the *Syiems* to administer justice. On the civil side, Section 19 states that the *Syiem's* Court can adjudicate any civil cases arising within its respective locality in which Khasis who reside or hold land within its respective locality in which the parties were Khasis. The Court of *Syiemship* includes the *Sirdar*, *Lyngdoh* or *Wahadadar*. With regard to non-Khasis, Section 20 further states that the Assistants to the Deputy Commissioner shall be the Court of first instance, except when the parties concerned invoke or submit to the *Syiem's* Court within its jurisdiction. The Deputy Commissioner or Additional Deputy Commissioner and his Assistants could not function as an original court in cases triable by *Syiem's* Court.[6]

In all civil matters, Section 23 states that the Deputy Commissioner or Additional Deputy Commissioner could adjudicate according to customary law wherever applicable, and where the customary law cannot be applied to either party it could, adjudicate, according to justice, equity and good conscience. The rules state that an appeal lies to the Deputy Commissioner or the Additional Deputy Commissioner from decision of the Assistants to the Deputy Commissioner and the *Syiem's* Court within thirty days and sixty days respectively of the date of the decision.[7]

In addition to the above order, the Governor of Assam also issued a Notification No.SK/140/49/9 dated 25 January 1950, directing that with effect from 25 January 1950, the reference to the "Dominion Agent, Khasi States", "Additional Dominion Agent, Khasi States", "Assistant to the Dominion Agent, Khasi States" and the "Court of the Khasi States Federation" wherever they occur in all enactments applicable to the Khasi States or Shillong Administered Areas under the Extra Provincial Jurisdiction Act, 1947, shall be construed respectively to the "Deputy Commissioner, Khasi and Jaintia Hills District", "Additional Deputy Commissioner, Khasi and Jaintia Hills District", "Assistant to the Deputy Commissioner, Khasi and Jaintia Hills District" and the "Court of the Deputy Commissioner, Khasi and Jaintia Hills District".[8]

Thus, with effect from 15 August 1947, there was no more political officer in the Khasi States. From 15 August 1947 to 25 January 1950, there was a Dominion Agent, Khasi States, and the Deputy Commissioner, Khasi and Jaintia District held the post, in addition to his own duties. But with effect from 26 January 1950, there was no more Dominion Agent, Khasi States. There remained only the Deputy Commissioner, Khasi and Jaintia Hills District.

Here, it may be noted that there had been a confusion between the terms "Khasi and Jaintia Hills District" and "United Khasi-Jaintia Hills District" as per Notification No.TAD/R/50/8 dated the 31st March 1951, published in the Assam Gazette dated 4 April 1951:

> "The Deputy Commissioner, Khasi and Jaintia Hills District, Additional Deputy Commissioner, Khasi and Jaintia Hills District, and Assistants to the Deputy Commissioner, Khasi and Jaintia Hills District are appointed respectively ex-officio Deputy Commissioner United Khasi-Jaintia Hills District, Additional Deputy Commissioner, United Khasi-Jaintia Hills District and Assistants to the Deputy Commissioner, United Khasi-Jaintia Hills District."[9]

The latter expression indicated that the Khasi States were a part of the United Khasi-Jaintia Hills District to differentiate it from the Khasi and Jaintia Hills District which were the erstwhile British territories.

In April 1952, in exercise of the power conferred by Paragraph 19 of the Sixth Schedule to the Constitution of India, the Governor of Assam issued a Regulation (Regulation III) known as the Assam Autonomous Districts (Administration of Justice) Regulation, 1952, issued under Notification No.TAD/R/11/51/106, dated 3rd April 1952 and published in the Assam Gazette, Part II-A, dated 9th April 1952. According to this Regulation No.III of 1952, necessary modifications were made in the Rules for the Administration of Justice and Police in the Khasi and Jaintia Hills, 1937, the Notification No.166-B dated the 16th March 1948, issued by the Ministry of States, Government of India, relating to Shillong Municipality;[10] the Khasi States (Application of Laws) Order, 1949, published with Notification No.SK/40/48/93 dated 1st June 1949 and the Khasi States (Administration of Justice) Order, 1950, published with Notification No.SK/140/49/8 dated 25th January 1950.[11]

In May 1952, by virtue of Paragraph 19 of the Sixth Schedule to the Constitution of India, certain amendments were brought into force in certain areas of the Khasi States vide Regulation-V known as "The United Khasi-Jaintia Hills District" (Application of Laws) Regulation, 1952 issued under Notification No.TAD/B/35/51 dated 6th May 1952 and published in the Assam Gazette, Part II-A dated 14th May 1952. According to this Regulation, the Governor of Assam may, by notification in the official Gazette, direct that any of the laws specified in the Schedule, shall extend to, and have effect, in so much areas of the United Khasi-Jaintia Hills District which were known as the Khasi States immediately before the commencement of the Constitution of India, and for this purpose different areas and different dates may be specified for different laws. The Regulation further provides that such laws in their applications to the Khasi States shall be subject to the same exceptions or modifications as they are subject to in the rest of the areas of the United Khasi-Jaintia Hills District.[12]

Then, on 12 December 1952, in accordance with the Khasi States (Application of Laws) Order, 1949, the Government of Assam in a letter to the Deputy Commissioner, United Khasi-Jaintia Hills directed that under the proviso to Paragraph 20(2) of the Sixth Schedule to the Constitution of India, the former Shillong Administered Areas should be excluded from the purview of the District Council in matters relating to village or town administrative including the establishment of village or town police.[13]

The formation of the United Khasi-Jaintia Hills Autonomous District Council in 1952 have eroded the *Syiem's* judicial power to a considerable extent. The judicial administration in the district was bifurcated between the Deputy Commissioner and the District Council and is based on (i) the Sixth Schedule to the Constitution of India, (ii) Rules for the Administration of Justice and Police in the Khasi and Jaintia Hills, 1937, (iii) the Khasi Syiemships (Administration of Justice) Order, 1950, and (iv) the Assam Autonomous Districts (Administration of Justice) Regulation, 1952 (Regulation No.III of 1952). However, during the pre-independence days and the period upto 1952, the judiciary was the exclusive sphere of the Deputy Commissioner who used to exercise his powers by himself and through his assistants. But in the post-independence days, after the formation of the Khasi Hills Autonomous District Council, the Sixth Schedule to the Constitution of India, envisaged a scheme whereunder the Khasi Hills Autonomous District Council exercises exclusive judicial powers in certain matters while in certain other matters, the Deputy Commissioner and his Assistants have been entrusted with the exercise of judicial powers.

Paragraph 4(1) of the Sixth Schedule to the Constitution of India, lays down rules for the administration of justice in the autonomous district and autonomous regions. It empowers the District Council or Regional Councils to constitute Village Councils or Courts for the trial of suits and cases between the parties all of whom belong to Scheduled Tribes within the areas of the District Council, subject to certain exceptions. This paragraph also authorises the District or Regional Councils to appoint suitable persons to be members of such Village Councils or Presiding Officers of such Courts. However, suits and cases between a tribal and a non-tribal party or among the non-tribal parties either of the district or outside come under the jurisdiction of the Courts of the Deputy Commissioner and his Assistants who exercise the power of Civil and Criminal Courts.

Paragraph 5 of the Sixth Schedule provides that cases involving offences punishable with death, transportation for life, or imprisonment for a term of not less than five years under the Indian Penal Code or under any other law for the time being applicable to such district, shall not be within the jurisdiction of the District Council Courts unless the Governor invests these Council Courts with the power to try the case. These cases, therefore, generally constitute the exclusive jurisdiction of the Deputy Commissioner's Court irrespective of the fact whether the parties involved belong to Scheduled Tribes or not. Thus, the Sixth Schedule has laid down a clear boundary lines between the judicial sphere of the two sets of Courts.

As regards the procedure to be followed in the trial of suits and cases in the Council Courts, Sub-Paragraph (3) of Paragraph 5 of the Sixth Schedule provides that the Code of Civil Procedure, 1908, and the Code of Criminal Procedure, 1898 (now 1973) shall not apply to the trial of any suits, cases or offences in an autonomous district to which the Sixth Schedule applies. Consequently, the District Council of the United Khasi-Jaintia Hills had formulated its own rules for administration of justice within the limits of the rules formulated by the Governor of Assam. In that new set up, the Deputy Commissioner's power was lost.

In 1953, as contemplated by Paragraph 4(4) of the Sixth Schedule to the Constitution of India, the Khasi Hills Autonomous District Council with the previous approval of the Governor of Assam framed the United Khasi-Jaintia Hills Autonomous District (Administration of Justice) Rules, 1953, duly notified in the Notification No.DC/LX/29/53 dated 18th December 1953. Under these Rules, the jurisdiction of the Deputy Commissioner's Court will no longer be available to suit and cases where the parties are tribal persons and have equivalent powers like the District and Sessions Judge and the District Council Magistrate has also sentencing powers of five to seven years as has been conferred upon them by the Governor of the State under Paragraph 5 of the Sixth Schedule to the Constitution, and where the cases are within the jurisdiction of the Courts constituted by the District Council.

Under the United Khasi-Jaintia Hills Autonomous District (Administration of Justice) Rule, 1953, there are three types of courts, namely, (i) Village Courts, (ii) Subordinate District Council Court and Additional Subordinate District Council Court, and (iii) District Council Court. The Rules, however, contain provisions for the Constitution, their powers and jurisdiction to try suit and cases. In the former Shillong Sub-division, there were 31 erstwhile British Village Courts which were known as British *Sirdarships* before the commencement of the Constitution. Above these Courts there is a Subordinate District Council Court at Shillong presided over by a Magistrate of the First Class who has unlimited original jurisdiction in respect of civil matters but limited jurisdiction in criminal cases. This court hears appeals from the 31 Village Courts. In the areas of the former Khasi States, above the Village Courts there are 25 additional Subordinate District Council Courts presided over by the *Syiems*, *Lyngdohs*, *Wahadadars* and *Sirdars*. These courts have unlimited civil, but limited criminal jurisdiction. They have been variously invested with powers of the Magistrate of First, Second or Third Class; and they hear appeals from the decisions of the Village Court within their respective jurisdiction.[14]

Before proceeding further, a detailed provisions of the judicial system in the Khasi Hills under the United Khasi-Jaintia Hills Autonomous District (Administration of Justice) Rules, 1953, may be made so as to enable us to know as to what extent the Khasi Hills Autonomous District Council could succeed in the administration of justice with regard to both civil and criminal cases where the parties to disputes are tribal persons.

The United Khasi-Jaintia Hills Autonomous District (Administration of Justice) Rules, 1953, was further amended by the Khasi Hills Autonomous District Council from time to time, for the better and smooth functioning of the Council in administering justice to the tribal people. The first amendment was amended by the Council on 9 December 1980. The Second amendment was passed on 13 March 1986, and the third amendment was adopted by the Khasi Hills Autonomous District Council on 17 March 1987.

The Constitution, powers and procedure of the three different classes of Courts are given below:

Constitution of Village Court

Rule 5(1) of the 1953 Rules states that there shall be a Village Court for each village. The rule as amended by the Second Amendment states that subject to the approval of the Executive Committee, there shall be a Village Court for each village. Provided that two or more villages may together form one village court; Rule 5(2)(a) states that each Village Court shall be composed of the recognised *Sirdar*, *Syiem Raid* (Bhoi), *Basan*, *Lyngdoh*, *Lyngskor* or headman of the village, Rule 5(2)(b) states that not less than two and more than six members and may be decided and elected by the majority of the village adults in an open *durbar* if such a member has not been fixed by practice or custom; but if the number has been fixed that number and these members shall continue if the number be more than six.

Rule 5(3) of the same Rules also states that there shall be a Chairman and a Vice-Chairman and a Vice-Chairman of each Village Court; Rule 5(3)(b) further states that the Chairman of the Village Court shall be the *Sirdar*, *Syiem Raid* (Bhoi), *Basan*, *Lyngdoh*, *Lyngskor* or headman or any such elected by the Village Court if there are more than one. Rule 6(3)(c) also states that the Vice-Chairman shall be one of the members of the Village Court elected by the majority of the members of the Court; and he shall perform the duties of the Chairman in his absence. Rule 4 further provides that there shall be a Secretary of the Village Court to be appointed by the Court from amongst the members of the Court. Rule 5 also provides that an elected member of the Village Court shall have a tenure of five years from the date of his first sitting in the Court but shall be eligible for re-election. Rule 6 also provides that the quorum of the Village Court shall be three members or one-third of the total number of members of such Court, whichever is greater. Rule 6(2) empowers the Secretary of the Village Court to record the proceedings of the Court. Rule 6(3) further states that the jurisdiction of a Village Court shall extend to the hearing and trial of suits and cases arising within the territorial limits of a village.[15]

Powers of Village Courts

Under the 1953 Rules, the Village Court is to try suits and cases of a civil nature; provided that if any immovable property is in dispute the property must be situated within the jurisdiction of the Village Court and in all other cases all the parties must reside or hold land within such jurisdiction. The Village Court can also try criminal cases falling within the purview of tribal laws and customs and offences of a petty nature such as petty theft and pilfering, mischief and trespass of a trivial nature, simple assault and hurt, affront and affray of whatever kind, drunkenness or disorderly brawling, public nuisance and simple cases at wrongful restraint.[16]

The Village Court shall have the power to impose a fine of Rs.50/- which was enhanced to Rs.150/- in 1986; payment in retribution or compensation to the aggrieved or injured party in accordance with the customary law. In civil cases, the Village Court shall have power to award all costs, as also compensation against vexation cases. Fines and payments may be enforced by attachment of property. Non-attendance of witnesses or any person wilfully failing to attend the Village Court may be imposed a fine of Rs.25/- which was enhanced to Rs.50/- in 1986. An appeal from the Village Court shall lie to the Subordinate District Council Court or the Additional Subordinate District Council Court.[17]

Procedure of Village Court

The 1953 Rules provide that a Village Court shall try all suits and cases in accordance with the customary laws of the village. It further provides that a Village Court shall try all cases in open *durbar* in the presence of at least three members and decide the issue by a simple majority of votes. After hearing both parties and witnesses, if any, it shall pronounce a decision. Provided that the President or Vice-President shall have a casting vote when there is a tie. A Village Court may pass an *ex-parte* decision if it is satisfied that the other party wilfully absents itself. Provided that if the adjournment is given on the motion of a party that party shall pay the adjournment cost not exceeding Rs.10/- to be appropriated to the District Council. The proceedings of a Village Court shall be recorded in writing. The Rule further states that a Village Court may carry out its decision or may order an attachment of property as soon as a judgement is pronounced, but if the property so attached is to be sold, the party concerned may appeal within sixty days, without the orders of the District Council.[18]

Constitution of Subordinate District Council Court and Additional Subordinate District Council Court

Rule 7(1) of the 1953 rules as amended by the Second Amendment Rules, 1986, states that there shall be a Subordinate District Council Court or Courts at Shillong for the whole of the Khasi Hills Autonomous District. Each Court shall be presided over by a Judicial Officer to be designated as Magistrate appointed by the Executive Committee with the approval of the Governor and such Judicial Officer shall also act as Recorder of the Court. In addition, there are also the Courts of the *Syiems*, *Lyngdohs*, *Wahadadars*, *Sirdars* or Administrative Officers as the Additional Subordinate District Council

Courts. The territorial jurisdictions of the Additional Courts are co-extensive with the *Syiemship*, *Lyngdohship*, *Wahadadarship* or *Sirdarship* as the case may be. Each such Additional Subordinate District Council Court shall be presided over by the *Syiem*, *Lyngdoh*, *Wahadadar*, *Sirdar* or Administrative Officer, with such number of *Myntris* (Ministers) or other customary elders determined by the Executive Committee of the District Council. Where there is more than one *Sirdar* or *Wahadadar* or any such elected by the members of the Additional Subordinate Court shall be the Presiding Officer. The Presiding Officer shall also act as a Recorder of the Court. The rules as further amended made a provision that the member of the Additional Subordinate District Court shall have a tenure of office of five years from the date of its first sitting of the Court but shall be eligible for re-election.[19]

The jurisdiction of the Subordinate District Council Court or other Courts of the District Council at Shillong shall extend to (a) suits and cases between parties residing within the jurisdiction of the different Village Courts in the whole of the Khasi Hills Autonomous District excluding the *Syiemships*, *Lyngdohships*, *Sirdarships* or *Wahadadarships* and to suits and cases which are not triable by such Village Courts, (b) suits and cases between parties residing within the jurisdiction of the different Additional Subordinate District Council Courts. On the other hand, the jurisdiction of an Additional Subordinate District Council Court shall extend to suits and cases not triable by Village Court in which all the parties reside within its territorial jurisdiction.[20]

Powers of Subordinate and Additional Subordinate District Council Court

Rule 17 of the 1953 rules, as amended in 1986, provides that a Subordinate District Court or Additional

Subordinate District Council Court shall exercise such powers as defined in Chapter III of the Code of Criminal Procedure, 1898, as it may be invested with by the Executive Committee of the District Council with the approval of the Governor.[21] Further, in exercise of the powers conferred by Rule 17 of the United Khasi-Jaintia Hills Autonomous District (Administration of Justice)Rules, 1953, the Executive Committee of the United Khasi-Jaintia Hills District Council, with the approval of the Governor of Assam, invests the following courts of the Council acting as Additional Subordinate District Council Courts under Sub-rule (2) of Rule 7 of the aforesaid rules with such powers of a Magistrate as noted against each and as defined in Chapter III of the Code of Criminal Procedure, 1898, to be exercised in their respective jurisdiction.[22]

	Courts		Powers
1)	The Court of the *Syiem* of Mylliem	1)	Powers of a Magistrate of the First Class
2)(a)	Courts of the *Syiem* of Nongkhlaw, Cherra, Khyrim, Nongstoin and Maharam *Syiem-ship*, and	2)	Powers of a Magistrate of the Second Class
(b)	the Court of the *Wahadadars* of the Shella Conferderacy.		
3)(a)	Courts of the *Syiem* of Nongspung, Langrin, Mawsynram, Myrïaw, Rambrai, Mawiang, Bhowal, Malai-sohmat, Nobosohphoh and Jirang *Syiemships*,	3)	Powers of a Magistrate of the Third Class.[23]
(b)	Courts of the *Lyngdohs* of Sohïong, Mawphlang and Lyngïong *Lyngdoh-ships*, and		
(c)	Courts of the *Sirdars* of Mawlong, Mawdon, Dwara-Nongtyrmen, Pam-sanngut and Nonglwai *Sirdarships*.		

However, the Subordinate District Council Court and the Additional Subordinate District Council Court are not competent to exercise jurisdiction in certain matters like Sections 124-A, 147, 153 and 193 of the Indian Penal Code; and Sections 107 to 110, 144 and 145 of the Criminal Procedure Code unless specially empowered by the Governor.[24] Therefore, suits and cases referred to the above rules shall continue to be tried and dealt with by the existing courts, that is, the court of the Deputy Commissioner and his Assistant, until such time as the Governor deems fit to invest the Subordinate District Council Court and Additional Subordinate District Council Court with such powers by Notification in the official Gazette. Further, whenever there is any likelihood of breach of peace or whenever any person accused of any offence involving a breach of peace or any person accused of committing criminal intimidation is convicted of such offence by any Court of the District Council and such court requires a person to execute a bond for committing the peace, the matter shall be referred to the Deputy Commissioner.

An appeal shall lie to the District Council Court from the decisions of the Subordinate District Council Court in any case, civil or criminal within sixty days of the date of order. The District Council Court may hear the appeal itself or may endorse it for hearing by the Additional District Council Court. In case the District Council Courts is not sitting, for some reasons, the appeal shall lie to the Additional District Council Court.[25]

So far as the procedures of the Subordinate District Council Court and the Additional Subordinate District Council Courts are concerned, the same will be discussed along with the procedures of the District Council Court.

Constitution of District Council Court

Rule 9 of the 1953 rules provides that there shall be one District Council Court for the United Khasi-Jaintia Hills Autonomous District which shall be called the United Khasi-Jaintia Hills District Council Court. The Court which shall ordinarily sit in Shillong shall consist of one or more judicial officers to be designated as Judge appointed by the Executive Committee with the approval of the Governor. The Court may also sit at any other place within the jurisdiction of the District Council in the public interest. Later on, in 1987, a provision was made for one Additional District Council Court for the Khasi Hills Autonomous District, which shall be called the Khasi Hills Additional District Council Court to be presided over by a judicial officer to be designated as Additional Judge. The Additional District Council Court also shall ordinarily sit at Shillong or at any other places within the jurisdiction of the District Council whenever it deems necessary in the public interest.[26]

Powers of District Council Court

Rule 29 of the 1953 rule, as amended by the first amendment rules, 1980, provides that the District Council Court shall be a Court of appeal in respect of all suits and cases triable by the Additional Subordinate District Council Court.[27] The District Council Court shall be competent to direct a Subordinate or Additional Subordinate District Council Court to try a civil suit which is not triable by such court. It further provides that the District Council Court may pass any order or appeal authorised by any law for the time being, in force. It also states that the District Council Court may call for and examine the records of any proceedings of a Subordinate District Council Court, and Additional Subordinate

District Council Court, or a Village Court and may enhance, reduce, cancel or modify any sentence or finding passed by such Court or remand the case for retrial. The District Council Court is further empowered to transfer a case or itself try it, or may act either on the report of the lower court or on the application of a party interested or on its own initiative.[28]

Procedure of the Subordinate District Council Court, Additional Subordinate District Council Court and District Council Court

Procedure in Criminal Cases

Rule 43(1) of the 1953 Rules as amended in 1986 lays down that in criminal cases the procedure of the Subordinate District Council Court, Additional Subordinate District Council Court and the District Council Court shall be in the spirit of the Code of Criminal Procedure, 1973, so far as it is applicable to the circumstances of the district, except summons on any person who resides outside the jurisdiction of the autonomous district or who does not belong to a Schedule Tribe shall be issued by the High Court, through the Deputy Commissioner of the District. Rules 45 also provide that in all cases, these three courts shall adjudicate according to law, justice, equity and good conscience and that the witnesses shall be examined on or solemn affirmation.[29]

Procedure in Civil Cases

In civil cases, Rule 47 of the 1953 rules as amended in 1986 and 1987, lays down that the procedure of the District Council Court, Additional District Council Court, Subordinate District Council Court or Additional Subordinate District Council Court shall be guided by the spirit, but not bound by the letter of the Code of Civil

Procedure, 1908, as amended up-to-date. The decree of the Appellate Courts in a civil case shall be transferred to the Court passing the original order for execution. Further the provision lays down that there shall be no imprisonment for debt, except in cases where the District Council Court or Additional District Council Court, Subordinate or Additional Subordinate District Council Court is satisfied that fraudulent disposal of property has taken place and detained for a period of six months.

Procedure for the Execution of Sentences, Decrees and Orders by the Different Hierarchy of Courts under the Khasi Hills Autonomous District Council

Rule 52 of the 1953 Rules states that whenever a Village Court has sentenced an offender to pay a fine in criminal case or passed an order for the payment of any money by a person in a civil suit, the Court may (a) issue a *parwana*, and (b) may apply, in writing, to the Chief Executive Member to realise the amount of execution according to civil process against the movable or immovable property.[30] As per Rule 53 of the same Rules, the Subordinate District Council Court, Additional Subordinate District Council Court, District Council Court or Additional District Council Court shall cause a sentence, order or decree in accordance with the procedure, prescribed by the Code of Criminal Procedure 1973 or the Code of Civil Procedure 1908, as amended up-to-date.[31]

Rule 53 lays down a procedure for the attachment of property. The rules as amended in 1986, states that a property, movable or immovable, belonging to the judgement debtor over which he has a disposing power to exercise for his own benefit, whether the same been held in the name of the judgement debtor or by another person on his behalf is liable to attachment and sale in execution of a decree, the procedure shall be in the spirit of the Code of Criminal Procedure, 1973, or the Code of Civil Procedure, 1908, as amended up-to-date. With regard to miscellaneous procedure, Rule 56 provides that whenever any court passes any order for the detention of a criminal lunatic the District Council shall refer the matter to the Deputy Commissioner, who shall deal with the case following the spirit of the Code of Criminal Procedure, 1973, and in accordance with rules framed by the Government of Meghalaya under the Indian Lunacy Act, 1912.[32] The Rules of 1953 are in force since 7 January 1954, as per the Notification No.DC/XXVI/8/53/102 dated 28 December 1953. However, as long as the United Khasi-Jaintia Hills Autonomous District (Administration of Justice) Rules, 1953, framed by the Council has not come into force, between the period from 1952 upto 6 January 1954, the United Khasi-Jaintia Hills District (Application of Laws) Regulation, 1952 (Regulation No.V of 1952) was adopted by the Council for administering justice in the Khasi Hills.

On the coming into existence of the District Council, the judicial powers in the autonomous area of the United Khasi-Jaintia Hills District, the tribal people were governed by the United Khasi-Jaintia Hills Autonomous District (Administration of Justice) Rules, 1953, framed by the District Council duly approved by the Governor of Assam. On its coming into force, on 7 January 1954, the *syiems* exercise their power under the said District Council Rules and the Justice Rules of 1950 and 1952 were repealed by Rule 58 of the said Rules, 1953, in so far as they related to the matters dealt with the said 1953 Rules. The *Syiem's* Court and the District Council Courts exercise judicial power and jurisdiction over all the Shillong Administered Areas except the areas comprised in the Shillong Municipality only as amongst the tribal people.

Since the District Council came into existence and after the enactment of the United Khasi-Jaintia Hills Autonomous District (Administration of Justice) Rules, 1953, different Courts were established under the said rules as discussed above.

High Court

Above the various Courts of the Khasi Hills Autonomous District Council lies the High Court. As to the High Court, on 16 January 1954, the Governor of Assam, acting under Paragraph 4(3) of the Sixth Schedule to the Constitution of India, issued the Assam High Court (Jurisdiction over District Council Courts) Order, 1954. The order is the material for ascertaining the position as to the appellate and revisional jurisdiction of the High Court of Gauhati as regards the Khasi and Jaintia Hills District.

Section 3 of the order empowers that an appeal against a final order or decision of District Council Court in a civil suit where the valuation of the suit is Rs.1,000 or more, shall lie to the High Court; provided that such appeal shall be presented within ninety days from the date of the order or decision appealed against. The order also empowers the District Council Court that in criminal cases an appeal shall lie to the High Court within sixty days from any order of conviction of the District Council Court awarding a sentence of six months imprisonment or upwards. In case of acquittal by the District Council Court an appeal must be presented within ninety days. The order further provides that the High Court may, on application or otherwise, call for the proceedings of any civil or criminal case decided by or pending in any court in the autonomous district constituted under the provisions of Paragraph 4(1) and (2) of the Sixth Schedule to the Constitution.[33]

In 1969, certain amendments were introduced in the Sixth Schedule with a view to (i) extending the jurisdiction of the tribal courts to non-tribal parties, (ii) taking away the appellate powers of the Regional Council and District Council, and (iii) also curtailing the powers of the Governor to confer the powers under the Civil Procedure Code and Criminal Procedure Code to these Courts. The object of these amendments was to enable these Courts to function more or less like Nyaya Panchayats as in the rest of the country and to make provisions for appeals from these Courts to regular Courts. These amendments were to come into effect on dates to be fixed by the President of India. However, till the time of writing the operative date has not been fixed due to some controversies relating to the power of the autonomous District Council and the position of the non-tribal people in the tribal area.

Supreme Court

The Supreme Court of India is the highest Court of Appeal in the country. It has also original jurisdiction over civil and criminal matters. All judgements from the Courts of the Autonomous District Council may be appealed against in the High Court and from the High Court to the Supreme Court both in regard to civil and criminal cases. Article 136 of the Constitution of India states that the Supreme Court in its discretion, grant special leave to appeal from any judgement, decree, determination sentence or order in any cause or matter passed by any court or tribunal in the territory of India; and Article 137 states that the Supreme Court shall have power to review any judgement pronounced or order make by it.[34]

As regards the powers of the Supreme Court to issue certain writs, Article 139 provides that Parliament may be law confer on the Supreme Court power to issue directions, order or writs, including writs in the nature of *habeas corpus*, *mandamus*, prohibition, quo warrant and *certiorari*, or any of them, for any other purposes. Article 141 further states that the law declared by the Supreme Court shall be binding on all Courts within the territory of India and article 142 also states that the Supreme Court in the exercise of its jurisdiction may pass such decree or make such order for doing complete justice in any cause or matter pending before it and shall be enforceable throughout the territory of India in such manner under any law made by Parliament and, until provision in that behalf is so made, in such manner as the President may by order prescribed.[35]

Notes and References

1. Shullai, L.G., *Ki Hima Khasi* (L.G. Shullai, Shillong, 1974), p.27.
2. Sangma, Jangsan, *Law of Administration of Justice in Meghalaya* (Jangsan Sangma, Tura, 1973), p.18.
3. *The Assam Gazette, Extraordinary*, No.SK/140/49/8 dated 25 January 1950, cited in F.n. 1, p.27; F.n. 2, p.30.
4. *Ibid.*, pp.27-35; *Ibid.*, pp.30-35.
5. *Ibid.*, p.30; *Ibid.*, p.37.
6. *Ibid.*, p.31; 38-39.
7. *Ibid.*, pp.31-32; 39-40.
8. *The Assam Gazette, Extraordinary*, No.SK/140/49/8 dated 25 January 1950.
9. Shullai, L.G., *Delightful Shillong* (L.G. Shullai, Shillong, dated 15 June 1990), pp.20-21.
10. Jangsan Sangma, F.n. 2, pp.47-48.
11. Shullai, L.G., *Ka Extra Provincial Jurisdiction Act, 1947, Bad Kiwei de ki Aiñ Hapoh ka Bri U Hynñiewtrep*, Series 1 (n.d.), unpublished, pp.3-4.
12. Notification No.TAD/R/35/51, dated the 6th May 1952,

Regulation No.V of 1952, the United Khasi-Jaintia Hills District (Application of Laws) Regulation, 1952, p.1.

13. Government of Assam, Tribal Areas and Development Department No.TAD/RCV/142/52 dated Shillong, the 12th December, 1952.
14. Government of India, Ministry of Home Affairs, *Report of the Commission on the Hill Areas of Assam 1965-66* (Government of India Press, New Delhi, 1966), pp.99-100.
15. *Assam Gazette, the United Khasi-Jaintia Hills Autonomous District Administration of Justice Rules, 1953*, No.DC/LS/29/53 dated the 18th December 1953 (Bani Press, Shillong, 1953), p.3.
16. *Ibid.*, p.5.
17. *Ibid.*, pp.5-6.
18. *Ibid.*, p.11.
19. *Meghalaya Gazette, Notification*, No.8, Part IV, dated 5 April 1986, p.34.
20. *Ibid.*, p.85.
21. F.n. 61, p.6.
22. *Government of Assam, Notification No.DC.XXVI/31/54/68*, dated the 21st January 1955.
23. The Court of Criminal Procedure, 1973, does not envisage Magistrate of the Third Class. However, since the Notification is invalid these courts are exercising judicial powers directly under the District Council Court System.
24. F.n. 15, p.6; F.n. 19, p.26.
25. *Meghalaya Gazette, Notification No.10*, Part IV, dated 14 May 1987, p.24; F.n. 15, pp.7-8.
26. *Ibid.*
27. *Meghalaya Gazette, Notification*, No.55, Part IV, dated the 19th December 1980, p.256.
28. F.n. 15, p.9.
29. *Ibid.*, pp.11-12.

30. *Ibid.*, p.13.

31. *Meghalaya Gazette*, No.10, 8 May 1986, p.37; F.n. 25, p.28.

32. F.n. 15, pp.15-16.

33. *Assam Gazette, The Assam High Court (Jurisdiction over District Council Courts) Order, 1954*, No.TAD/R.11/53/23, dated the 16th January 1954, p.1.

34. *The Constitution of India (As amended up-to-date)*, (Allahabad Law Agency, Allahabad, 1987), pp.40-42.

35. *Ibid.*, p.43.

8

ADMINISTRATION OF JUSTICE IN KHASI HILLS (A CASE STUDY)

Before proceeding further, to see how far the District Council in Khasi Hills has been able to administer justice to the tribal people, an organisation of Court System for the Khasi Hills Autonomous District Council is given below to enable us to understand the hierarchical system of courts within the jurisdiction of the District Council. The organisational chart is as follows:

Organisation of Court System for the KHADC

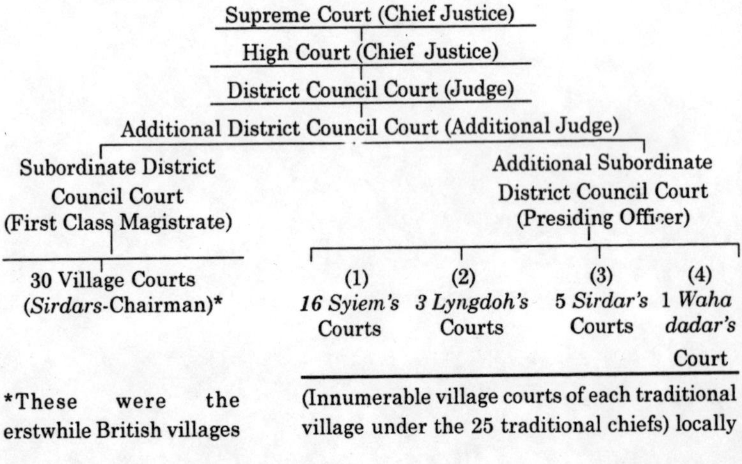

locally known as *Ki Hima Sorkar* to differentiate them from the traditional villages under the 25 Khasi States. Originally, there were 31 British villages but under the Khasi Hills Autonomous District (Administration and Election of *Sirdars* of Wahlong) Act, 1985, which was passed on 4 July 1985, and got the Governor's assent on 1 September 1985, the two villages of Byrong and Mawthangsoh-Khyllung *Sirdar-ship* were united together under one village of Wahlong *Sirdarship.* called *Ki Hima Syiem, Lyngdoh, Sirdar* and *Wahadadar* presided over either by a *Basan* and *Syiem Raid* (Bhoi) of the village. These administrative heads act as Chairman in their respective village courts. As per Circular *Purwana* No.DC/XXVI/36/54/85/10883-908 dated 5 August 1954, from the Office of the Executive Committee, United Khasi-Jaintia Hills District Council, there were 352 village courts. The latest figure is 248 village courts. The reduction in number of village courts is due to either their abolition or their becoming dysfunctional.[1]

Some representative cases of both civil and criminal cases tried at the different classes of the District Council Court during the period under study have been selected. The various types of cases which have been selected for study right from the lower level to the higher level are cases relating to alleged trespass; cases relating to title suit; cases relating to civil suit, that is cases relating to the inheritance of the ancestral property; miscellaneous case; miscellaneous criminal case; miscellaneous appeal; divorce cases and cases relating to civil special jurisdiction.

The selected cases which came up before the District Council Court right from the lower court, that is, the Village Court to the highest court, that is, the Supreme Court are given below. Real names involved in different representative cases not given for privacy protection.

First of all, we will take up the case presided over by

the *Sirdars* in the Village Court. In Khasi Hills, the *Sirdars* in the 31 erstwhile British villages act as the administrative heads in the village and as Chairman in the Village Court. In Khasi Hills, there were 31 Village Courts in the areas which were known as British *Sirdarships* before the commencement of the constitution. But from 15 April 1989, with the passing of the Khasi Hills Autonomous District (Administration and Election of *Sirdar* of Wahlong) Act, 1985, on 4 July 1985, and got the assent of the Governor on 1 September 1985, there are only 30 Village Courts with the Union of Byrong *Sirdarship* and Mawthang-Sohkhyllung *Sirdarship* into the Wahlong *Sirdarship*. These 30 villages are Jyrngam, Lakadiang, Laitkroh, Laitlyngkot, Marbisu, Mawbeh-Larkhar, Mawmluh, Mawsmai-Nongthymmai, Mynteng, Myrdon, Nongbah, Nongjri, Nonglang, Nonglait, Nonglynkien, Nongpoh, Nongriangsi, Nongriat, Nongshluid, Ramdait, Saitsohpen, Sinai-Mawshynrut, Sohbar, Synnei, Tynriang, Tynrong, Tyrna, Umniuh-Tmar and Wahlong *Sirdarships*. Out of these 30 villages, Marbisu *Sirdarship* is the selected Village Court for our study because it was found that Marbisu *Sirdarship* is one of the *Elakas*[2] (Administrative Unit), which had the longest service of administration for forty years under one *Sirdar*, late Mr. Hai Singh Sun. This selection, therefore, was made on the basis of a larger number of cases passed and disposed of by the Village Court. The selected case for study from the Marbisu *Sirdarship* is:

U Mr. A, *Rangbah Shnong* (Headman), W village – *Nongmudui* (Complainant)

Pyrshah (Versus)

U Mr. X, Z village – *Shahmudui* (Defendant)

Fact of the Case

The prosecution fact of the case was that on 31 August

1984, the complainant Mr. A, Headman of W Village in Marbisu *Elaka*, while coming back from the Mawngap market, saw the defendant Mr. X of Z Village in Marbisu *Ekaka* stealthily entered the complainant's house from the back side. Immediately, on seeing Mr. A, he ran and fled away to his own house. Looking at that very moment at his own house, the complainant, Mr. A found that part and portion of his house was damaged. Wherein the defendant Mr. X could manage to enter the house by taking out the plain sheet (*tin*) and the corner stone (*maw khrum*) on which the house was built. The defendant, after entering inside the house, first locked the house from inside and then made a thorough search in the house. The complainant, as the owner of the house was greatly shocked to see that the very same person had attempted the alleged theft several times. He found that his house was damaged by the defendant and that a bag of potatoes of about 50 kg was stolen away by him.

On such a crime being committed, the complainant on 3 September 1984, lodged a complaint to the Secretary, members and representatives of the local *durbar* of W Village, to the effect that the accused, Mr. X had committed the alleged theft, causing damage to his house and that also a bag of potatoes of about 50 kg was lost. Over and above circumstance, the complainant prayed the Secretary, Mr. Y of the local *durbar*, to take immediate action in the matter.[3]

On receiving the plaint from the complainant, the Secretary of the local *durbar* of W Village, convened a local *durbar* on 25 September 1984, requesting all the villagers to attend the *durbar*. On such a request, the villagers of the W Village assembled together on that day and the *durbar* made them known about the alleged theft being committed by Mr. X of Z village. The local *durbar*, after hearing the arguments from both sides of the contending parties, could not decide the matter, because while the complainant said that he had detected the defendant entering his house, the defendant denied of having committed such a crime. In the meantime, the *durbar* advised both the contending parties to compromise which was not accepted by the parties. Since, no decision could be arrived at, therefore, the local *durbar* transferred the case to the *Sirdar* of Marbisu and prayed him to settle the case. At the same time, the *Durbar* also requested the *Sirdar* of Marbisu for immediate disposal of the case and not to keep it pending, because there was a threat from both the parties.[4]

Immediately, on receiving the report from the Secretary of the local *durbar* on 27 September 1984, the *Sirdar* of Marbisu, late Mr. SS, served a *Purwana* to the complainant and the defendant to appear before him on 2 October 1984, at 10.00 a.m. The *Sirdar* also informed both the parties to bring along with them a *durbar* fee of Rs.20/- each for an enquiry.[5]

As per the *Purwana* issued by the *Sirdar* on 2 October 1984, both the contending parties appeared before the *Sirdar* of Marbisu. After making an enquiry, the *Sirdar* of Marbisu village found that the complaint of Mr. A, headman of the W village dated 3 September 1984, and the report from the Z village was a genuine one. Thereafter, the *Sirdar* and his *durbar* felt that it would be proper to make an enquiry in the Mawpun Rum village on 13 October 1984. The *Sirdar* also fixed the rate, and the cost for enquiry would be Rs.125/- each from both the complainant and the defendant.[6]

Points for Decision

The following are the charges framed for deciding the case.

1. Whether the enquiry conducted on 13 October 1984, could prove the alleged theft by the defendant or not?
2. Whether the defendant had entered and damaged the house of the complainant or not?
3. Whether the defendant had attempted the alleged theft or not?

Points Decided

1. That the enquiry made by the *Sirdar* on 13 October 1984, proved that the alleged theft being committed was a genuine one.
2. That the defendant had entered and damaged the back side of the complainant's house.
3. That the defendant had committed the theft.

Judgement and Reason for Decisions

The Village Court, Marbisu Village, after making an enquiry opined as follows:

With regard to the first point, the Village Court and its *durbar* found that the defendant, Mr. X pleaded guilty. The Village Court held the view that this was evident from the enquiry made on 13 October 1984, in the Z Village.

With regard to the second point, the Village Court found that the back side of the complainant's house was damaged by the defendant. It was also found that a sum of money was taken by him. After the agreed arrangement between the Chairman and its *durbar*, the Village Court held the view that the defendant had to pay a fine of Rs.500/- each to the *Sirdar* and to the village durbar.

With regard to the third point, the Village Court found that the defendant had stolen away a bag of potatoes of about 50 kg and kept it at the backside of the house. The court, however, felt that its *durbar* were of the opinion that the defendant, Mr. X had to pay a fine of Rs.300/-

each of the *Sirdar* and to the local *durbar* of the Mawpun Wah village.[7]

On the basis of the above findings and decisions, the court further held the view that the defendant would have to abide by further terms and conditions. If Mr. X, the defendant was again found to have been committing the same crime, then he would have to pay a fine of Rs.2,000/- to the village and that he had to leave the village for good. That the payment of fine of Rs.2,000/- had to be met by the defendant, Mr. X's relatives. If the payment of fine was not paid by his relatives, then the whole family of Mr. X would have to bear the consequence of leaving the village.[8]

After hearing the arguments from both sides of the contending parties and after a proper enquiry and examining the report from the Secretary of the local *durbar*, X Village, the Chairman of the Village Court, Mr. SS and his *durbar*, passed the judgement in favour of the complainant on 13 October 1984, and the case was disposed of accordingly.[9] An appeal from the 30 Village Courts lie to the Subordinate District Council Court.

In addition to 30 Village Courts, there are number of Village Courts under the 25 Khasi states. In addition, these 25 Khasi States were administered by the traditional chiefs recognised as *Syiemships*, *Lyngdohships*, *Sirdarships* or *Wahadadarships* being an area within the jurisdiction of a court. The decision of a Village Court was appealable to the Court of the *Syiem*, *Lyngdoh*, *Sirdar*, or *Wahadadar* concerned, within their respective jurisdiction.

By way of illustration, Raid Mawbah Village Court, under the Mylliem *Syiemship*, Umroi is a selected Village Court within the 25 Khasi States for study. This Court has been selected as the records of the selected case are available. Other Village Courts may also have other cases which records are not readily available. The selected case from this Village Court is civil case No.1 of 1981.

Ka Ms. B of N village, Raid Mawbuh–*Nongmudui* (Complainant)

Pyrshah (Versus)

Ka Ms. E of M village, Mylliem Syiemship – *Shahmudui* (Defendant)

The case was about the claim of the right of ownership over the disputed land at Umshyngiar, East Khasi Hills District.

Facts of the Case

The fact of the case was that the complainant, Ms. B was the daughter of late Ms. K. Late K was the adopted child (*Rap ïing*) of late J, the grandmother of the complainant. She took possession of the *Raid* (commune) land which comprised also a portion of the land set fire to it by Mr. C, according to the boundary submitted in the plaint. According to the plaint petition, the complainant stated that she got the land from late J as her adopted child. That the land was a *Raid* land which comprised a portion of the land set on fire by Mr. C. Further, the plaint petition stated that the complainant took possession and taken care of the land in dispute since the time of the death of late J. There was nobody to disturb or claim the land in dispute till the day that the land in dispute was set on fire on 14 February 1981.[10]

The complainant filed a plaint petition before the Village Court on 25 June 1981.[11] On the basis of the written statement by the defendant on 6 July 1981,[12] the complaint submitted a show cause petition on 21 July 1981, to make known about the plaint. On the basis of the show cause there was no claim from the defendant's side. Again on 14 August 1981, the complainant submitted the amended plaint before the Village Court, *Raid* Mawbuh. Later, on

24 August 1981, the defendant filed the additional written statement before the Village Court, *Raid* Mawbuh for confirmation of the case.[13]

Points for Decision

Over the pleadings of both the contending parties and after filing the documents, the Village Court, *Raid* Mawbuh, framed five issues for decision of the case.[14]

Whether the complainant has a cause of action to file a case?

Whether the case can proceed in this manner without making Mr. C a party to the case?

1. Who took possession of the land in dispute?
2. Who has got the right over the land in dispute?
3. What are the other reliefs the parties are entitled to get?

Points Decided[15]

1. That the complainant had a cause of action to file a case.
2. That the case can be proceeded without Mr. C, as a party to the case.
3. That the defendant took possession of the land in dispute.
4. That the complainant has got no right over the land in dispute.
5. That the parties were relatives and had to bear their own cost.

Judgement and Reasons for Decision

The lower court after framing the issues opined as follows:

With regard to Issue No.1 the lower court found that the learned lawyers of both the contending parties did not press or raise any arguments on this issue. The lower court, however, found that both the parties claimed the right of ownership over the disputed land. On the basis of findings, the lower court decided that the complainant had a cause of action for the case. Thus, the complainant won on this one count.[16]

Regarding Issue No.2 the lower court, found that the learned lawyers did not press or open the case regarding the setting on fire of Mr. C over the disputed land in their pleading. The court, however, found very clearly that the complainant wanted to confirm the right of ownership over the disputed land. On the basis of these findings, the lower court, therefore, decided that the case could be proceeded without making Mr. C a party to the case.[17]

With regard to Issue No.3, the lower court, held that from the pleadings of the witnesses of both the complainant's and the defendant's sides, it appeared clearly to the court, that the complainant had a case on the Exhibits 1, 2, 3 and 4 which were the documents renting out trees. As per evidence, the lower court found that these documents did not properly point out where the cultivation or felling of trees was done. The Court, however, found that the complainant's witness No.6 (P.W. No.6) stated that the disputed land was the O and the undisputed land was one portion of land at O and P. Considering the facts and the circumstances of the case, the court held the view, that unless these documents clearly indicated the boundaries or the witnesses clearly stated the boundaries of any portion of land, these documents or the witnesses were useless. The Court, however, pointed out that it could not ascertained which portion of the plot of land related to O which was renting out for cultivation or felling of trees. From these evidences, the court could not accept that it was the complainant who took possession of the disputed land. Further, from the documents filed by both the contending parties, the lower court found that the documents filed by the defendant's party carried more weight than the documents filed by the complainant's party. The court further held the view, that the witness No.2, Mr. G of the defendant's party further confirmed the proof stating that the land in dispute was taken possession by the defendant. On this basis, the court found that the witnesses could not be set aside in cross examination. The lower court, also found that the witness No.2 stated clearly that the defendant took possession of the land since the death of Mr. H and uptil now. On the basis of the above findings, the lower court, found that it was the defendant who took possession of the disputed land and thus the defendant won on this count.[18]

Regarding Issue No.4, the lower court sent their own people for local enquiry into the disputed land. However, the members of the court went on local enquiry on 24 August 1985, and submitted their report. According to the report, it appeared clearly to the lower court that there was a mounted portion (*kynton*) which demarcated the land in dispute and the land of Mr.G which extended upto the land of the XY. The court, further held the view that after having thoroughly examined the documents and after hearing the arguments of the witnesses over the dispute, the lower court, found that the complainant had got no right over the land in dispute. On the basis of the above findings, the court decided that it was the defendant who had got the right over the disputed land.[19]

Lastly, with regard to the Issue No.5, the lower court found that both the parties were relatives as kith and kin. Therefore, the court decided that both the contending parties had to bear their own expenses.[20]

This civil case No.1 of 1981 has come up for a final hearing before the Chairman of the Village Court, Mr. F along with three *Basans* of the court, Mr. A, Mr. B and Mr. C on 23 December 1985. The Chairman, accordingly after the evidence was adduced and after hearing the arguments of the learned lawyers and the witnesses from both sides of the parties, passed the judgement in favour of the defendant, Ms. E of M village and the case was disposed of without cost.[21]

Above the Village Courts of the 30 villages (erstwhile British villages) and the 248 traditional villages, there are 25 Additional Subordinate District Council Courts, presided over by the *Syiems*, *Lyngdohs*, *Sirdars* and *Wahadadars*. Of these 25 Khasi States, 16 are *Syiemships*, presided over by the *Syiems*, three *Lyngdohships* presided over by the *Lyngdohs*, five *Sirdarships* presided over by the *Sirdars* and one *Wahadadarship*, presided over by the *Wahadadar* under the Shella Confederacy.

Firstly, we will take up the case presided over by the *Syiems*. Out of 16 *Syiemships*, Mylliem *Syiemship* is selected because it is the only *Syiemship* in Khasi Hills which got the power of the first class magistrate to preside over the cases which have come up before the court. The case which we have taken up for study is Suit No.4 of 1978.

Mr. SR of LM village – *Nongmudui* (Complainant)

Pyrshah (Versus)

Mr. TS, LN village	
	Shahmudui (Defendants)
Ms. WN, LN village	

This case refers to a title suit over the position of a plot of land at YN in East Khasi Hills of Meghalaya.

Facts of the Case

The fact of the case was that the complainant (*Nongmudui*), Mr. SR owned a plot of land at YN, which he had purchased from Ms. K on 19 April 1976, who in turned had purchased the land from late Mr. W, his daughter-in-law as per the boundaries given in the plaint. Ms. K had acquired the land from late Mr. W after paying the full amount of the latter's expenses for the land. The payment of expenses (*siew bai nonglut*) was written in the sale deeds by Ms. K and late Mr. W. These documents were handed over to the complainant on his payment for the expenses for the land by Ms. K. Late Mr. W had a son, LN and a daughter, SN. The complainant, Mr. SR, on coming to know of the illegal possession of the said land by the defendants, the son and daughter of late Mr. W, sent a registered letter on 20 April 1978, to the defendants informing them that their father had already sold his lands to Mr. SR. He therefore asked them that they should not trespass and do any work in that land. At the same time, he also asked them to vacate the land and not to enter by force.[22]

After the defendants failed to comply with his letter, Mr. SR filed a petition on 19 May 1978, before the Presiding Officer, Additional Subordinate District Council Court, Mylliem *Syiemship*.[23] Against the plaint petition, the defendants in their written statement before the Court, on 29 August 1978, denied that there was any such sale as claimed by the complainant.[24] Hence, they denied the right of the complainant over the three lands at YN including the land in dispute. Hence the suit is for the declaration of right and title as well as for the eviction and permanent injunction to respective parties.[25]

Points for Decision

Over the pleadings of both the contending parties along with four witnesses from the complainant's side and five witnesses from the defendant's side, the court framed as many as seven issues in the suit for decision and judgement.[26]

1. Whether the defendants have a cause of action for this suit?
2. Whether the suit can proceed in this manner?
3. Whether the father of the defendants had a right to transfer the occupancy right of the suit land by documents dated 20 April 1974?
4. Whether the documents dated 19 April 1976 can stand?
5. Who is in possession of the land in dispute?
6. Whether the land in dispute is a *Ri Raid* land?
7. The other relief the parties are entitled to get?

Points Decided

1. That the defendants had a cause of action for the suit.
2. That the suit can be proceeded.
3. That the *Ri Raid* land according to customary law cannot be sold and purchased as in the case of self-acquired property, except as payment against expenses.
4. That the documents dated 19 April 1976 were genuine.
5. That the land in dispute was in possession by the complainant and that the defendants had used the said land by force.
6. That the land in dispute is a *Ri Raid* land.
7. That the defendants had to vacate the land since the land in dispute belongs to the complainant.[27]

Judgement and Reasons for Decision

The trial court after framing the seven issues for judgement and decision opined as follows:

Firstly, regarding issues No.1 and No.2 which relates to law and facts, the trial court found that since the defendants had not pressed on these issues, therefore, the court decided that the complainant had a cause of action for the suit. The trial court also held the view that since the case was conducted on the pleadings of both the parties, therefore, the complainant won on these counts.[28]

With regard to Issue No.3, the trial court held the view that in the pleading it was contended that according to the prevailing customary law, *Ri Raid* land cannot be sold and purchased like the self-acquired property. But the said land can only be given as payment of expenses. The trial court, further found that Ms. K paid the amount of expenses to late Mr. W wherein he also handed over the documents on payment of expenses from Mr. S and late Mr. W to Ms. K. The trial court also found that the amount of expenses for the land at YN which included "A", "B" and "C" had been paid by Mr. SR to Ms. K. Moreover, the court found that the witness was not challenged by the defendants that the documents were false. Therefore, the court felt that if late Mr. W could pay the amounts of expenses for the land to Mr. S, so also Ms. K could pay the amount of expenses to late Mr. W. Thus, the court decided that the documents dated 20 April 1974, were genuine which had also been confirmed by Ms. K.[29]

Regarding issues No.4 the Court held the view that the documents which were confirmed and corroborated by the seller, Ms. K was not challenged by the defendants. Thus, the trial court and its *durbar* found that the documents dated 19 April 1976 were genuine.[30]

With regard to Issue No.5 the trial court found that as

it appeared from the arguments of the complainant the defendants had trespassed into his land, for which a notice had been served by him to them that they could no longer use the land. It was further appeared that instead, the defendants continued using the land, having no regards to the notice issued by the complainant. It, therefore, appeared to the court that the physical possession of the land in dispute was in the hands of the defendants using it by force. Thus, the court and its *durbar* felt that the land in possession by force by the defendants could not give them justice.[31]

Regarding Issue No.6, the Court found that both the contending parties agreed that the land in dispute was a *Ri Raid* land.[32]

Lastly, with regard to Issue No.7, the trial court found that the land in dispute was a land for which the expenses had been paid by the complainant. Therefore, the court held the view that the defendants should vacate the said land. The court also directed the defendants not to disturb the right of the complainant or any of his family members.[33]

This suit No.4 of 1978 had come up for a final heraing before the Presiding Officer, Mr. Franciswell Syiem and his *durbar* on 10 April 1984. The Presiding Officer, accordingly after the evidence was adduced and after hearing the arguments of the learned lawyers from both sides of the parties, passed the judgement decreeing the suit in favour of the complainant, Mr. SR and the case was disposed of. However, the contending parties had to bear its own cost. The judgement was announced on 25 May 1984, and delivered on 4 June 1984.[34]

Next, we will take up the cases presided over by the *Lyngdohs* in the Additional Subordinate District Council Courts. The *Lyngdohs* act as the Presiding Officers in the above courts and as *Lyngdohs* in the *durbar*. It is to be noted that the courts of the *Lyngdohships* exercised their powers of a Magistrate of the Third Class as per Notification No.DC.XXVI/32/54/68, dated 21 January 1955, approved by the Governor of Assam, even though the code of Criminal Procedure 1973, does not envisage Magistrates of the third clas. Out of three *Lyngdohships*, Mawphlang *Lyngdohship* has been selected, because through investigation and information, we found that the court of Mawphlang *Lyngdohship*, is one of the Additional Subordinate District Council Courts which had tried as many cases at the Additional Court level, while in the other two courts of *Lyngdohships* the cases are only of administrative nature. The selected case from Mawphlang *Lyngdohship* which we have taken up for study is Civil Suit No.4 of 1974.

Ms. A of M village – *Nongmudui* (Complainant)

Pyrshah (Versus)

1. Mr. P		-	*U Shahmudui* (Defendant)
2. Ms. Q	of Mawphlang		
3. Ms. R	Mawphlang,	-	*Ki Shahmudui* (Co-Defendants)
4. Ms. S	Lyngdohship		
5. Mr. T			

The above case refers to a Civil suit over the position of a big plot of land and houses including the *Ïing niam* literally, a religious house, at Mawphlang in the East Khasi Hills District. The question for determination in this case was about the right of ownership over a landed property and physical possession of the lands and houses situated over the land of the ancestral property of late Mrs. BH the great grandchild of the complainant and the defendant No.1.

Facts of the Case

The fact of the case according to the plaint, was that late Mrs. BH who had a big plot of land at NG, had four daughters according to genealogical table in paragraph one of the plaint.

The four daughters of Mrs. BH were Mrs. C, Mrs. D, Mrs. E and Mrs. F. The youngest daughter had no daughter. Hence, succession would devolve on the third daughter. But Mrs. E's daughter, Mrs. M had no children. The next succession should have devolved, as per Khasi custom, to the successors of the second daughter of Mrs. BH, that is, Mrs. D's daughter – N, and grand-daughter – O.[35]

On the basis of the facts mentioned above, the complainant, Ms. A, on 26 February 1974, filed a plaint petition before the Additional Subordinate District Council Court, Mawphlang *Lyngdohship* stating that Ms. A was the youngest great grand-daughter of late Mrs. BH of Mawphlang *Lyngdohship*. That according to Khasi custom, she was the guardian of *Ka iing niam* (religious house) and other landed property of late Mrs. BH, as per the genealogical table submitted by her. She further stated that late Mrs. BH had a big plot of land and house including a religious house. The complainant alleged that Ms. A had been living in Shillong with her children, and in her absence, the defendant No.1, Mr. P sold two plots of land to each of the defendants No.2 and No.3, Ms. Q and Ms. R. The two plots of land were settled on rental basis for the teashops to defendants No.4 and No.5, Ms. S and Mr. T without the knowledge and consent of the complainant, Ms. A, who was the *Khadduh* (youngest daughter). When the complainant came to know about the transactions without the knowledge of the court of the *Lyngdoh* of Mawphlang and without the consent of the

Khadduh (Ms. A) felt that it was highly illegal and it was contrary to the customary law of the Khasis. The plaint petition further stated that the sale of land and the settlement of rent without the knowledge and consent of the *Khadduh* (Ms. A) was contrary to the customary law of the Khasis and it was, therefore, highly illegal.

Following the plaint petition of the complainant, on 25 March 1975, the defendant No.1, Mr. P. submitted a written reply before the court of the *Lyngdoh* of Mawphlang, against the plaint petition. In their written statement, the defendant pointed out to the court, that the plaint petition given by the complainant should not be accepted;[36] and that they did not want to file a case in the court.[37] Since, the plaint did not fix the value of the lands and houses and that the court fee stamp was not affixed according to the rules of the court.

Points for Decision

Over the above pleadings and issues given by both the complainant and the defendant No.1, the trial court framed as many as six issues for judgement and decision.[38]

1. Whether the complainant has a cause of action for this plaint?
2. Whether the houses and land at Mawphlang according to the sketch belong or not to the ancestral property kept by late Mrs. BH, the great grandmother of the complainant and defendant No.1?
3. Whether the genealogy of the complainant and the defendant No.1 as shown in the plaint was correct or not? If so, whether the complainant Ms. A was the youngest great grand-daughter who should inherit the ancestral property of late Mrs. BH?
4. Whether the defendant No.1 has got the right or not to intermeddle (*mushlia*) or sell or lease any plot of

the land or the ancestral house of late Mrs. BH? If so, whether the sale of the plots of land to the defendants No.2 and No.3 was legal and lawful and whether these transactions should be declared null and void?

5. Who bore the expenses for the funeral of late C?
6. What are the rights that the contending parties should get?

Points Decided[39]

1. That the complainant has got a cause of action to file a case.
2. That the houses and land at Mawphlang according to the sketch map belonged to the ancestral property of late Mrs. BH because the defendant No.1 did not contest on this point.
3. That the genealogy of the complainant and the defendant No.1 was correct since the defendant did not contest this point in his written statement. Moreover, that the complainant was the youngest great grand-daughter of late Mrs. BH who inherited her property.
4. That the defendant No.1 has got no right to sell the ancestral property. According to the Khasi customs, he can only lease the land and use all the produce from the ancestral land for the needs of his children.
5. That the defendant No.1 bore the expenses for the funeral of late Ms. C and that the complainant had not contributed anything.
6. That the selling of land by the defendant No.1 to the co-defendants No.2 and No.3 was legal and it will stand. That the defendant has got the right to maintain and take care of the house and landed property in his life time. Since the defendant had taken actions without the knowledge of the clan members, he should

be deprived of his right of enjoyment of the ancestral property in question.

Judgement and Reasons for Decision

The trial court after framing the above issues and after hearing the arguments of the three witnesses from the complainant's side and six witnesses from the defendant's side opined as follows.

Regarding Issue No.1, the court found that through the discussions of both the contending parties, the complainant has got cause to file a case, since the male members of the clan has no right to transfer immovable property.[40]

With regard to issues No.2 and No.3 the trial court found that the defendants did not contest this point.

Regarding Issues No.4 and No.5, the trial court held that to be the *Khadduh* (youngest daughter) was not an easy matter according to Khasi custom. The court held the view that the *Khadduh* goes together with the responsibility because during illness of any member of the family clan, the *Khadduh* should take the responsibility whether physically or in financial matters. Since the youngest daughter did not look after the needs of the family members, the trial court confirmed the sale of land and the renting out of shops by the defendant No.1 for maintaining the requirements of the ancestral family including the case of his grand-mother.[41]

Lastly, with regard to Issue No.6, the Court and its *durbar* after considering the matter felt it necessary that since the complainant did not show any concern in the misery of life and death of late C, the trial court decided that the selling of land to the defendants No.2 and No.3 will stand. However, the court held the view, that the ancestral property should be transferred to the complainant from the date of issuing the judgement. That the defendant No.1 should surrender the ancestral property to the complainant and that the defendants No.4 and No.5 and all those who had let out on rent within the ancestral property should pay the rent to the complainant.[42]

The case has come up for final hearing before the Presiding Officer, Mr. Z and his *durbar* on 21 January 1978. The Presiding Officer, after adducing evidence and after hearing the arguments of the learned lawyers from both the complainant and the defendant No.1 passed the judgement in favour of the complainant, Ms. A and the case was disposed of on 29 April 1978, with no cost.[43]

The next category of court case taken up for study is the one taken up over by the *Sirdars* in the Additional Subordinate District Council Court. The *Sirdars* act as the Presiding Officer in the above court and as *Sirdars* in the *durbar*. In Khasi Hills, the courts of the *Sirdarships* exercised their powers of a Magistrate of the Third Class as per Notification No.DC.XXVI/31/54/68, dated 21 January 1955. However, as mentioned earlier, the Code of Criminal Procedure, 1973, does not envisage magistrate of the Third Class. Out of 25 Khasi States, there were five *Sirdarships* in Khasi Hills. Out of these five, Mawdon *Sirdarship* has been selected because through information received from the District Council Court, Khasi Hills Autonomous District Council, Shillong, Mawdon *Sirdarship* has been one of the *Sirdarships* in which appeal has come up before the judge of the Khasi Hills District Council Court against the judgement passed by the Additional Subordinate District Council Court, Mawdon *Sirdarship*. The selected case for study is Title Civil Appeal No.1 of 1983.

Mrs. C, LM, Shillong-2 – *Nongappil* (Appellant)

Pyrshah (Versus)

1. Mrs. J - *Shahappil* (Respondent)
2. Mr. W

Baroh arngut na XY
Sirdarship (Both from XY,
Mawdon *Sirdarship*)

The instant appeal was regarding the judgement dated 20 October 1983, passed by the Village Court of Mawkhan village in Title Suit No.1 of 1981 wherein the petition dated 31 January 1981, of the appellant was dismissed.

Facts of the Case

The fact of the case was that the appellant Mrs. C was the daughter of late Mrs. SK who had kept a number of grove (*bri*) for her children. After the death of late Mrs. SK in 1970, their children had divided the land/grove among themselves. One of the divided lands was the HK (R) and according to the partition of the grove (*bri*) HK belongs to the appellant. Because the appellant resided at Shillong, working as a government servant, she was not in a position to manage the grove by herself. Therefore, the grove (*bri*) HK (R) had been managed by the appellant's elder brothers, Mr. O and Mr. P. On 6 October 1980, when Mr. O died, the grove (*bri*) was managed by Mr. P. After the former's death, in the month of November 1980, an information was received by the appellant that the respondents went to clear (*mait*) the *Bri* HK. When the respondents who were the wife and son of Mr. O were asked not to do so, they instead threatened them, by revealing that they wanted to take possession of the grove and that too to claim as the right of ownership over the land.[44]

This claim of the right of ownership over one grove

(*bri*), led the appellant along with her brother Mr. P by a plaint petition dated 31 January 1981, to the *Sirdar* of Mawdon, Mawdon *Sirdarship* (but not before the Presiding Officer, Additional Subordinate District Council Court, Mawdon *Sirdarship*). This petition in question was transferred by the *Sirdar* of Mawdon *Sirdarship* to the Village Court of Mawkhan to try the case and to do the needful by his order dated 3 April 1981. On 20 October 1983, the Mawkhan Village Court decreed the suit in favour of the respondents.[45]

Being highly aggrieved at and dissatisfied with the impugned judgement and orders of the Village Court, on 28 November 1983, the appellant preferred an appeal before the Presiding Officer, Additional Subordinate District Council Court, Mawdon *Sirdarship*.

Points for Decisions

The Presiding Officer, Mr. F, Additional Subordinate District council Court, Mawdon *Sirdarship*, had framed four issues for decision of the case.[46]

1. Whether this land was given by the appellant for management to Mr. O, husband of the respondent or was it the land possessed by Mr. O for himself and his wife, the respondent No.1?
2. Whether the boundaries of the disputed land support the case of the respondents/opposite party?
3. Whether a copy of the partition deed of the grove dated 5 January 1971, as submitted by the appellant can be substantiated?
4. Whether the respondents had threatened the appellant/complainant as alleged?

Points Decided[47]

1. That the land/grove in dispute was the land possessed by late Mr. O and his wife the respondent No.1.

2. That the boundaries of the disputed land could not be ascertained from the respective parties. But it was clear that part of the boundaries of the land in dispute at *Bri* HK as given by both the parties were the same.
3. That the photostat copy of the appellant's partition deed could not prove that there was a partition of the said land among brothers and sisters of the appellant.
4. That there was no need to enquire or examine the matter mentioned in the appeal such as the alleged threat by the respondent to the appellant.

Judgement and Reasons for Decisions

With regard to the first issue, the trial court found that the land in dispute was possessed by the respondent and there was nothing to show that the land/grove was possessed or managed for somebody else except for Mr. O and his wife the respondent No.1. The court on its findings held the view that there was nothing to show that the land was kept for the appellant.[48]

Regarding the second issue, the court found that the boundaries given by the appellant did not comply with the boundaries given by the respondents. But the trial court, after a cross-examination on the question of boundaries, found that parts of the boundaries given by both sides of the parties were the same. Therefore, on the basis of findings the court held that there was no doubt that the land in dispute was the grove (*bri*) HK on which the contending parties claimed for it. However, the trial court replied in the affirmative, that the boundaries as per the findings of the court did not support one side on the other in the dispute.[49]

With regard to the third issue, the court held upon that it could not accept the mere photo copy of the partition deed and that there was no evidence to prove the partition of the landed properties among brothers and sisters of the appellant. Even so, the trial court after reading the photo copy of the partition deed particularly on the partition of the landed properties among children carefully, found that the appellant had four brothers and sisters and that Mr. O, the husband of the respondent No.1 was one of them. The court also found that there was nobody to give witness on the partition of the landed properties. On these findings, the court held the view, that there was nothing on the records to show that there was the original copy of the partition of the land among the children. Therefore, the court could not accept this particular point in the appeal petition. Thus, on this issue, the trial court rejected the claims of the appellant.[50]

With regard to the fourth issue, the trial court felt that it was not necessary to enquire or re-examine the case relating to the alleged threat by the respondents against the appellant. On this point, the court held the view, that according to their findings, it was very clear that the Village Court Mawkhan, had done it according to law. That the Village Court, had recorded the reply of the witnesses, had examined thoroughly the documents and heard the arguments of the parties. The trial court held the view that it had found no reason as to why the case should be reviewed or to begin it anew.[51]

This case has come up for the final hearing before the Presiding Officer, Mr. F on 21 March 1984. The Presiding Officer, after thoroughly going through the documents and after carefully examining the case records of both the contending parties, found that the appeal had no foundation and therefore it was rejected.[52] Thus, the trial court passed the judgement in favour of the respondents on 23 March 1984, and the case was disposed of without cost.[53]

The last court in the category of 25 Khasi States is the *Wahadadar* court of the Shella Confederacy. This court is presided over by the *Wahadadars* of Shella Confederacy in the Additional Subordinate District Council Court. The Court of the *Wahadadars* of the Shella Confederacy exercised their powers of Magistrate of the second class as per Notification No.DC.XXVI/31/54/68, dated the 21 January 1955, approved by the Governor of Assam. The *Wahadadars* of Shella Confederacy acts as the Presiding Officer in the above court and as *Wahadadar* in the *durbar*. The selected case from the *Wahadadar* of Shella Confederacy is Misc. Case No.11 of 1979.

Mr. E, K village – *Nongai Dorkhast*
(Complainant)

Pyrshah (Versus)

Mr. T of L Bazaar – *Shah ai Dorkhast*
(Defendant)

Facts of the Case

The fact of the case was that Mr. R of L granted a periodical and renewable lease of a plot of land at W Bazaar to late Mr. Y to construct a shop thereby executing a sale deed dated 21 September 1950, and granted receipt-accepting rent for five years. Thereupon, late Mr. Y constructed a shop on the said plot of land. On 5 June 1953, late Mr. Y sold his shop by executing a sale deed to late Mr. S, father of Mr. T of L Bazaar for Rs.950/- and late Mr. S took possession of the shop. On 1 November 1955, late Mr. R renewed the lease of the plot of land with late Mr. S. He accepted land rent for five years and granted a receipt with renewable clause. After the death of late Mr. R, the complainant, Mr. E his uncle inherited his property and renewed the lease of the plot of land with late S and accepted land rent for eleven years amounting to Rs.55/- and granted receipt on 27 January 1974. However, from the date of purchase, late Mr. S was in possession of the shop with his son Mr. T and reconstructed the shop. After his death, his son Mr. T being the legal heir of his father inherited the shop and resided therein.[54]

On 24 December 1979, the complainant, Mr. E filed a petition before the trial court stating that Mr. T, son of late Mr. S deserted the shop situated in Shella Bazaar which land belongs to the complainant. At the same time he also heard that the defendant wanted to sell the shop. But as his father did not regularly pay the rent, therefore, he prayed the trial court not to allow him to sell or lease or do anything to the house.[55]

On receiving the plaint from the complainant, the trial court served the *purwana* to Mr. T to appear before the court and later Mr. T's petition was accepted. Before the case was tried by the Court on 20 June 1982, it was decided earlier that Mr. T should be prevented from selling the shop till the case was disposed of by the Court.

Points for Decision

The Court framed the following issues for a decision.[56]

1. Whether the prohibition order issued by the Court to Mr. T holds good forever against him or not?
2. Whether the complainant, who owned a land at L Bazaar had the power and rights to hold the house situated on his land?
3. Whether the defendant had showed to the Court that he had come to his wits end to contest the case?
4. Whether the defendant had got the rights to claim the shop in L Bazaar?
5. Whether the selling of shop by the defendant was against the contempt of court order or not?

Points Decided[57]

1. That the prohibition order issued by the Court to Mr. T holds good forever against him.
2. That the complainant, the inhabitants of L, who had owned land in L Bazaar, had the power and rights to hold the house situated on his land and it was his property.
3. That as Mr. T could not substantiate the case before the court and left L, it showed to the court that he had come to his wit's end to contest the case.
4. According to the *ex-parte* judgement, the court gave its decision in favour of the complainant and justified that the defendant had no right whatsoever to claim the shop in L Bazaar.
5. That the action of Mr. T against the decision of the court by selling the shop as appeared in his petition dated 28 September 1980, was treated by the court as the "contempt of court order" which deserved severe punishment.

Finally, the trial court after hearing the arguments from one side only, came to the conclusion that the right of selling of the shop by Mr. T was rejected. The selling of the shop could not be accepted, as it appeared to the court that the act of such selling was a deceitful case. Thus, the court passed the *ex-parte* judgement in favour of the complainant, Mr. E on 5 December 1980, and that the complainant should bear his own cost.[58]

The next hierarchy of Court to be discussed here will be the court presided over by the Magistrate First Class of the Subordinate District Council Court, Khasi Hills District Council Court. The selected case from this court is Misc. C.R. Case No.1 of 1987.

Mrs. C of M village, – Petitioner
LM, Shillong

(Versus)

Mr. TK, N village – Opposite Party
R.E. Division, M.S.E.B., N village

This is a case on application made under Section 125 Cr.P.C. by the petitioner, Mrs. C for the maintenance of her minor children by her husband, the opposite party, Mr. TK which has been registered as Misc. Criminal Case No.1 of 1987.

Facts of the Case

The case in brief was that the petitioner, Mrs. C was the legal wife of the opposite party, Mr. TK and out of the matrimonial alliance with the opposite party, the petitioner had four children, namely (1) U WS (son) aged 11 years, (2) Ka XS (daughter) aged 10 years, (3) Ka YS (daughter) aged 8 years, and (4) Ka ZS (daughter) aged 6 years. In August 1980, the opposite party, Mr. TK deserted the petitioner, Mrs. C and her children in 1985, and since then neglected to properly maintain his children. On the demand of the petitioner, the opposite party occasionally gave Rs.200/- or Rs.300/- to his children. But the opposite party did not give money every month and at times he refused to pay maintenance to the children since 1985. After the desertion, the opposite party in 1985 committed adultery with Ka KK of OP and lived with her as husband and wife at V, Shillong. The opposite party, U TK was working as a Junior Divisional Accountant in the Office of the Executive Engineer, O R.E. Division, drawing a salary of Rs.2,348.34 in the summer and Rs.2,408.34 in the winter. Under these circumstances, on 22 April 1987, the petitioner filed a petition to the court that the opposite party had neglected to maintain his legitimate children who were living with her. She, therefore, prayed the court that the opposite party be ordered to pay a monthly allowance of Rs.400/- for each of his children.[59]

Points for Decision

The Presiding Officer, Subordinate District Council Court, Mr. JN, framed five issues for the case.[60]

1. Who can be ordered to pay maintenance in this case?
2. Whether the opposite party is the father of the minor children for which maintenance has been prayed for?
3. Whether the children for which maintenance has been claimed are minors, unable to maintain themselves?
4. Whether the opposite party has sufficient means to maintain his minor children?
5. Whether the opposite party neglected or refuses to pay maintenance for his minor children?

Points Decided[61]

1. That the father of the children can be ordered to pay maintenance for his minor children.
2. That the opposite party was the father of the children for which maintenance has been claimed.
3. That the opposite party admitted that his children from the petitioner were minors.
4. That the opposite party has sufficient means to maintain his minor children.
5. That the opposite party has never maintained his children as the petitioner has never claimed for that.
6. Four more additional points included that the opposite party was liable to pay maintenance allowance for his minor children.
7. That the opposite party should pay Rs.200/- per month to each of his four minor children as maintenance allowance.

8. That the amount of maintenance should be paid to the petitioner being the natural guardian of the minors and that payment should be made before 15th of every month.
9. That monthly allowance should be payable with effect from the month of June 1988.

Judgement and Reasons for Decision

The court after framing the above issues opined as follows:

Regarding the first issue for consideration, the court found that a bare perusal of Section 125(1)(b) Cr.P.C. makes it clear that the father of the minor children can be ordered to pay maintenance for his minor children.[62]

With regard to Issue No.2 upon the facts found by the court, was that the opposite party in his show cause did not deny that he was the father of the minor children. The court also found, that in cross-examination the opposite party had stated that he and the petitioner lived together as husband and wife publicly and that the petitioner had four children by him. In view of this position, the court therefore admitted that the opposite party was the father of the minor children for which maintenance has been claimed.[63]

With regard to Issue No.3, the court found that the opposite party had never challenged the fact that his children from the petitioner were minors who were unable to maintain themselves. In view of this non-denial of the opposite party as to the age of the petitioner's children, the court answered the question referred to it in the affirmative.[64]

Regarding Issue No.4, the court found that the opposite party had never challenged about his monthly income of more than Rs.2000/- per month. The court also found that the opposite party's pay at the time of trial was Rs.2500/-. Thus, the court held the view that the opposite party had sufficient means to maintain his minor children.[65]

With regard to Issue No.5, the court found that the opposite party had not only admitted his negligence or refusal but also shown his liability to pay maintenance for his children. The court was, therefore, constrained to answer this point in the affirmative.[66]

This case has come up for final hearing before the First Class Magistrate, Mr. JN on 18 April 1988. Accordingly, after the arguments of the learned lawyers from both sides and after carefully going through the case records and considering the earning capacity of the opposite party, the court ordered the opposite party to pay Rs.200/- per month to each of his four children before the 15th of every month as maintenance allowance. The payment would come into effect from June 1988. Thus, the court passed the judgement in favour of the petitioner, Ka C of M village. The judgement was delivered on 17 June 1988, and the case was disposed of without cost.[67]

Above the Subordinate and Additional Subordinate District Councils is the Additional District Council Court presided over by the Additional Judge. The selected case from this court is Misc. Appeal No.1 of 1989.

U CD and others - Appellants

(Versus)

Ka GY - Respondent

This is the miscellaneous appeal directed against the Order dated 27 February 1989, passed by the Additional Subordinate District Council Court of Khyrim Syiemship in Misc. Case No.7 of 1988, granting temporary injunction to the Respondents.

Facts of the Case

The fact of the case was that the respondent Ka GY, instituted a title suit in the Additional Subordinate District Council Court, Khyrim *Syiemship* for the declaration of right, title and for permanent injunction of the actual and physical possession over a plot of land at K under U *Syiemship*. On 2 August 1988, the respondent, ka GY, filed a petition before the Court praying for the temporary injunction to cultivate her land at K under U village *Syiemship* against the Appellant, U CD.[68] Later on, the trial Court made the *ad-interim* injunction granted absolute.[69]

The appellant, U CD, being highly aggrieved by and dissatisfied with the order of the trial court, on 7th April 1989, appealed to the District Council Court to set aside the impugned order of the trial Court and also prayed the Court to stay the operation of the lower court's order pending the disposal of the appeal.[70] The District Council Court subsequently handed the case to the Additional Judge of the Additional District Council Court.

Points for Decision

On these pleadings, the following are the issues framed for decision of the case.[71]

1. Whether the land in dispute is under the attachment order passed by the Magistrate?
2. Whether the respondent granted permission to cultivate and possess the land in dispute by the *Sirdar* of U village?
3. Whether the boundaries of the disputed land are given in the attachment order?
4. Whether the attachment order was a final order in the case?
5. Whether the attachment order had been executed or not?

Points Decided

1. That the land in dispute was not under attachment.
2. That the respondent had been granted permission to cultivate and possess the land by the *Sirdar* of U village.
3. That no boundaries of the disputed land were given in the attachment order.
4. That the attachment order was not a final order.
5. That the attachment order had not been executed.[72]

Judgement and Reasons for Decision

With regard to the first issue for consideration, the court found that the appellant could not produce any documents to show that the land was under attachment.

Regarding Issue No.2, from the records, the court found that the respondent was granted permission to cultivate and possess the land in dispute by the *Sirdar* of U village by a document dated 1 June 1988, and that the boundaries of the disputed land had been clearly defined in the said document.[73]

With regard to Issue No.3, the court held that after examining the attachment order of the Magistrate, Shillong, in City Case No.20 of 1974, attached in the records, the court found that the name of the disputed land was vague and no boundaries of the disputed land were given in the attachment order.[74]

Regarding Issue No.4, the court found that the attachment order passed on 21 August 1974, appeared not to be a final order in the case. The court, further held upon that on having examined the same order, it showed that the order was yet to be executed and that the matter was still pending before the Magistrate, Shillong.[75]

With regard to Issue No.5, the court found that the

appellants could not produce any other documents to show that the attachment order had been executed and that the land in dispute was therefore, under the attachment order of the Magistrate, Shillong.[76]

This miscellaneous appeal has come up for a final hearing before the Additional Judge, Mr. JN of the Additional District Council Court on 15 September 1989. Accordingly, after hearing the arguments of the learned lawyers for both the parties and carefully going through the records and in view of the above findings, the Additional Judge, saw no merit to interfere with the order dated 27 February 1989, of the lower court of Khyrim *Syiemship* granting temporary injunction. The Additional Judge, accordingly dismissed the appeal without cost and the judgement was delivered on 16 November 1989.[77]

The next court to be taken up for study is the one presided over by the Judge, in the District Council Court. The selected case from this court is Divorce Suit No.8 of 1988.

Ka MB,	–	Petitioner
XY village		
	(Versus)	
1. KD,	–	Respondent
OP village		
2. Ka PN	–	Co-Respondent
OP village		

Facts of the Case

The case in brief was that the petitioner, Ka MB and the Respondent, U KD were husband and wife. Prior to the solemnisation of the marriage between them, the respondent and the petitioner had stayed together as husband and wife in the year 1965. Thereafter, the marriage between them was regularised and solemnised on 18 May 1966 by the licenced church at NK village at the house of the petitioner. At the time of regularisation and solemnisation of the marriage, the petitioner was already pregnant from the respondent and the first child was born on July 1966. After the solemnisation of the marriage, the petitioner lived together with the respondent as husband and wife at XY village, at the house of the respondent's parents. Out of the said union, five children were born. On account of some misunderstanding with the parents of the respondents, sometime in September 1980, the respondent, U KD deserted the petitioner without any reasonable cause and went to stay with his elder brother at ST village. In January 1981, the respondent committed adultery with Ka PN, the co-respondent at OP village. Out of the said adulterous union, two children were born. The respondent himself informed the church that he had committed adultery, whereby the church ex-communicated him.[78]

Due to the act of adultery committed by the respondent, the petitioner, Ka MB, did not want to take back the respondent as husband. The petitioner, had obtained the marriage certificate given by the church, but the same was lost. Accordingly, a certified copy of the effect of her marriage to the respondent was given by the licenced church of the Presbyterian Church. Under the above circumstances, the petitioner on 9 September 1988, filed a petition before the court of the Judge, and prayed the court to admit her petition and to pass order for the dissolution of marriage.[79]

Points for Decision

On the basis of an application for the dissolution of marriage, the following are the points for decision.[80]

1. Whether the petition for divorce is admissible or not?
2. Whether it is possible for the petitioner to stay with the respondent as husband and wife?

Points Decided[81]

1. That the petition for divorce is admissible.
2. That it was no longer possible for the petitioner to stay with the respondent as husband and wife.

Judgement and Reasons for Decision

The court after framing issues opined as follows.

With regard to the first point, the court found through the records that the respondent himself informed the church of the said act of adultery whereby the church ex-communicated him.[82]

Regarding the second point, the court found that the petitioner had not condoned the said Act of adultery committed by the respondent. But the court held the view that the petitioner and the respondent last resided together at XY village, within the jurisdiction of this court. Further, the court also found that there was nothing to show that any collusion or connivance existed between the petitioner and the respondent in filling the instant suit.[83]

This case has come up for a final hearing before the Judge of the District Council Court, Mr. R on 10 July 1989. On the above facts and circumstances of the case and from the evidence of records, the Judge was therefore, satisfied to allow the petitioner for divorce and the marriage between them was dissolved. The case was disposed of and the same was yet to be confirmed by the High Court.

Beside the above cases presided over by different classes of courts of the District Council, there are also other representative cases relating to the Khasi Hills Autonomous District Council which came up before the

Gauhati High Court. The selected case from this Court is (Civil Special Jurisdiction) Civil Rule No.629 of 1980.

Shri Jidon Singh Syiem	-	Petitioner
(Versus)		
The Executive Committee, District Council, Khasi Hills and others.	-	Respondents

Facts of the Case

The fact of the case was that Shri Jidon Singh Syiem, Deputy Chief (*Syiem Khynnah*) of Langrin *Syiemship* in Khasi Hills filed a petition in the Gauhati High Court, Shillong Bench on 17 December 1980, challenging the order of the Executive Committee, Khasi Hills District Council dated 24 October 1980, in Memo No.DC.XXVII/ 47/ Gen/80/44 deciding to take recourse to Section 14 of the United Khasi Jaintia Hills Autonomous District (Appointment and Succession of Chiefs and Headmen) Act, 1959. According to Section 14 of the Act, the Executive Committee of the Council took over the administration of the Langrin *Syiemship* from U Doli Singh Syiem, the *Syiem* of Langrin *Syiemship* due to his prolonged illness and appointed an administrative officer on 25 October 1980.

The petitioner in his petition showed that he was appointed as a member of the Langrin *durbar* in 1933 and worked with late Borba Singh, who was the *Syiem* at that time of the *Elaka*. In 1955, the *Elaka durbar* of the *Syiemship* (Langrin *Elaka*) appointed the petitioner as a Deputy *Syiem* of Langrin *Syiemship* by the order of the *Syiem* dated 14 May 1955. The petition, stated that in paragraph 1 of the order it was described that he would shoulder the duty of the Executive administration and administration of justice of the *Elaka* along with the *Syiem*, the *Myntris* and the *durbar* in every respect and in paragraph 2 it was described that he would be one of the officers of the *Elaka* and in paragraph 3, it was described that in case of death of the present *Syiem*, u Doli Singh Syiem, would immediately take over the duty of the *Syiem*. The petition further stated that the Act was passed in pursuance of Part II of the Sixth Schedule to the Constitution of India by the District Council of the United Khasi-Jaintia Hills District which had received the assent of the Governor of Assam on 16 October 1959.[84]

Further, the petition stated, that after the Act came into force on 16 October 1959, the respondent No.4, u Doli Singh Syiem wrote to the Chief Executive Member, District Council United Khasi and Jaintia Hills, Shillong, on 18 October 1959, for confirming the petitioner as Deputy Chief of the Langrin *Elaka* and the KHADC also gave its assent to his appointment on 8 March 1969. The petitioner, thereafter, continued to serve as the Deputy Chief and on the removal of the *Syiem* of Langrin due to his ill health, the petitioner was appointed Acting *Syiem* on 23 July 1971.[85] Subsequently, u Doli Singh Syiem and his *Myntris* and elders proposed to the KHADC on 4 October 1980, to appoint an administrator instead of an acting *Syiem*.[86] Accordingly, the KHADC appointed an administrator, Shri Belking Star Syiemïong on 25 October 1980.[87] This was against the interest of U Jidon Singh Syiem, the petitioner who filed the petition to the High Court.

Points for Decision

The following are the points for decision.[88]

1. Whether the petitioner was appointed by order No.DC/MPC/55/68/9/2471, dated 8 March 1969, for the post of Deputy Chief in Langrin *Syiemship*?
2. Whether the impugned order dated 24 October 1980, was purely an administrative order?

3. Whether the petitioner was appointed as Deputy Chief under Section 10 of the Act?
4. Whether the period of such taking over will also affect the functions and duties already delegated by the Chief to the Deputy Chief?
5. Whether the petitioner has got the right to challenge the order?
6. Whether the District Council has got the right to take over the administration of the *Elaka*?
7. What are the qualifications of the person to be appointed as an administrative officer?
8. Whether the petitioner was a member of the Durbar and the Deputy Chief of the Durbar?
9. Whether the petitioner as the Deputy Chief had been affected by the impugned order?

Points Decided[88]

1. That the petitioner was appointed as Deputy Chief by order No.DC/MPC/55/68/9/1471, dated 8 March 1969, under Section 10 of the Act as amended.
2. That the impugned order dated 24 October 1980, was purely an administrative order.
3. That the petitioner was appointed as Deputy Chief under Section 10 of the Act.
4. That there was nothing in the Act which was intended to alter past rights which were vested before the Act came into operation.
5. That the petitioner had got the right to challenge the impugned order.
6. The petitioner's contention that the District Council has no right to take over the administration of the *Elaka* under Section 14 of the United Khasi & Jaintia

Hills District Council (Appointment and Succession of Chiefs & Headmen) Act, 1959, seems to be without any force, in view of the ruling in T. Cajee V. U Jormanik Siem, AIR 1961 S.C. 276.[90]

7. That the administrative officer may also be appointed from among the persons who are headmen or elders of the *Elaka*.
8. That the petitioner was still a member of the *durbar* and the Deputy Chief of the *Durbar*.
9. That the petitioner as the Deputy Chief had not been affected by the impugned orders.

Judgement and Reasons for Decision

We shall now confined ourselves to analysing the judgement of the High Court.

Regarding the first point for determination, the Hon'ble High Court was of the opinion that the petitioner was appointed by the order of the Executive Committee of the Council dated 8 March 1969, as the Deputy Chief under Section 10 of the said Act as amended. As such, he might be said to have been reappointed under the said section and had possessed his rights and duties as such. The Hon'ble High Court found that being the Deputy Chief he performed the duties and bore the responsibility with the *Syiem* in the duties and functions delegated to him.[91]

With regard to the second point for consideration, the Hon'ble High Court found that the impugned order was purely an administrative order. But the High Court held upon that it would be too wide a proposition to say that an administrative order could never confer or take away any right.[92]

With regard to the third point, the Hon'ble High Court found that the petitioner was appointed as Deputy *Syiem* under Section 10. As such, the Court held the view that he must be supposed to have been continued to be vested with the powers conferred upon or delegated to him by the *Syiem* with the approval of the District Council.[93]

Regarding the fourth point, the court found that there was nothing in the Act which was intended to alter past rights which were vested before the Act came into operation. On such findings, the court held the view that under Section 10(1) of the Act, a Deputy Chief may be removed from his office by the Chief and his *durbar* with the previous consent of the Executive Committee. On this basis, the court found that no such step was shown to have been taken. Without any expressed provision in the enactment, the court held upon that the petitioner might not have been divested of power, rights and duties. Therefore, the Court opined that the petitioner had not been removed and so in no way been affected by the impugned orders.[94]

Regarding the fifth point, the High Court held that even if the impugned orders were otherwise found to be contrary to or not in accordance with law, the court found that the petitioner as a member of the *Elaka*, shall have the right to challenge the order.[95]

With regard to the sixth point, the High Court found that the petitioner's contention that the District Council had no right to take over the administration of the *Elaka* under Section 14 seems to be without any force, in view of the ruling in T. Cajee vs. u Jor Manik Syiem, AIR 1961 S.C.276. On the basis of this finding, the High Court held the view that it was very clear that the Chief had been examined by the State Standing Medical Board, Meghalaya, which reported on 26 August 1980, that the *Syiem*, u Doli Singh, had been suffering from a degenerative mental disease. He was irrelevant and memory confabulation was severely lost. Regarding this report, the Court therefore, replied that this was the finding of fact by an expert body and as such it might not be opened for the court to interfere with the finding.[96]

With regard to the seventh point, the High Court found that the statute provides that such an administrative officer may also be appointed from among the persons who are headmen or elders of the *Elaka*. On this basis of findings, the court held upon that this was indicative of the power to appoint anyone who was neither a headman nor an elder member of the *Elaka*. In this view of the matter, the court held that even though the respondent No.5, u Belking Star Syiemiong was not hitherto a member of the *durbar*, he could not be held to be disqualified from being appointed as an Administrative Officer. The objection on this ground by the petitioner was rejected by the High Court.[97]

With regard to the eighth point, the court found that the administrative officer, under the impugned order dated 24 October 1980, was to be assisted by the existing *Myntris* and the *Elaka* in the administration. The court also found that the order allowing the *Myntris* to run the administration temporarily as conveyed in DC No.XXVIII/Gen/137/79/2 dated 7 November 1979, had been withdrawn. On the basis of these findings, the High Court held that under Section 14 of the said Act, the Executive Committee was empowered to appoint an administrative officer together with either the Chief's Durbar of the Committee consisting of four to six members appointed by the Executive Committee to assist the administrative officer in running the administration of the *Elaka* as the case may be. As such, the court was of the opinion that there could be no doubt that the petitioner was still a member of the *Durbar* and the Deputy Chief of the *Durbar*.[98]

With regard to the last point for decision, the Hon'ble High Court held the view that those functions and duties already delegated to the petitioner and having not specifically withdrawn by the *Syiem* in *Durbar*, those continued to be vested in him might not be affected. As such, the High Court was of the opinion that the petitioner as the Deputy Chief had not been affected by the impugned orders.[99]

This Civil Special Jurisdiction has come up for a hearing before the Hon'ble Mr. Justice, K.N. Saikia, of the High Court, Shillong Bench, on 2nd, 3rd and 4th April 1981. Accordingly, on 6 May 1981, the Hon'ble Judge, after hearing the arguments of the learned Councels, from Mr. K.P.Sen for the petitioner and Mr. S.C. Das appearing for the District Council held that there was no merit in this petition and therefore, the petition filed by the petitioner was rejected and without cost.

Apart from the cases which have come up for judgement and decisions before the Courts of the KHADC and the Hon'ble Gauhati High Court, there are also other representative cases relating to the Khasi Hills Autonomous District Council matters which came up before the Indian Supreme Court. The selected case for study from this Court is Civil Appellate Jurisdiction, Special leave petition (Civil) No.8394 of 1987.

Bara Bazar Merchants and Shop Keepers' Association, Bara Bazar, Shillong - Petitioner

(Versus)

Khasi Hills District Council, Shillong and others - Respondents

This is a petition under Articles 132 and 136 of the Constitution of India filed by the petitioner for Special leave to the Supreme Court from the judgement and order passed by the Hon'ble Gauhati High Court dated 12 June 1987, in Civil Rule No.425 of 1975.

Facts of the Case

The fact of the case was that the petitioner was a member of the Association of Merchants, Shopkeepers and Traders, who had been doing business in Bara Bazar, Shillong. The Association had been registered under the Registration of Societies Act, 1860. All the members of the petitioner's association were citizens of India. Many of them were non-tribal traders and some members of the Association belong to the tribal community. That in the purported exercise of its power conferred by paragraph 10 of the Sixth Schedule to the Constitution, the respondent framed a Regulation called United Khasi-Jaintia Hills District (Trading by Non-Tribals) Regulation, 1954. That under the provisions of the Regulations, a system of taking out a licence by the non-tribal people before doing any business within the jurisdiction of the District Council had been provided. Subsequently, with the approval of the Council, the Executive Committee of the District Council framed rules called the United Khasi-Jaintia Hills Autonomous District (Trading by Non-Tribals) Rules, 1959. That the object and purpose underlying the enactment of the Regulation was merely to levy fees on the non-tribal traders in the district. The petition of the petitioner, however, submitted that the regulation did not disclose as to what services, if any, were rendered by the District Council so as to justify the levy of fees on the non-tribal traders of the district. That the rules prescribed various different fees for carrying out different types of business.[100] The petition of the petitioner, however, submitted that the regulation did not disclose as to what services, if any, were rendered by the District Council so as to justify the levy of fees on the non-tribal traders of the district. The petitioner was very much aggrieved over the Rules and Regulations of the KHADC and petitioned the Gauhati High Court for redress.[101] The High Court, however, did not give any relief to the petitioner in its judgement on 12 June 1987.[102]

Thereafter, the petitioner challenged the judgement and order of the Hon'ble High Court. The petitioner in the appeal petition to the Hon'ble Supreme Court of India in July 1987, prayed the Hon'ble Supreme Court to grant special leave to appeal from the judgement and order of the High Court dated 12 June 1987, in Civil Rule No.424 of 1975 and to pass such orders as the court deems fit and proper in the interest of justice.[103]

On August 1987, the petitioner filed an application petition for special leave to appeal from the order passed by the High Court on 12 June 1987. The petitioner, however, prayed leave to the Hon'ble Supreme Court to treat the contents of the special leave petition as part and parcel of the application. The petitioners further submitted that the impugned order was wholly erroneous in law based on the earlier judgements of the Supreme Court. The petitioner, also submitted that irreparable loss, injury and prejudice would be caused to the petitioner unless the Supreme Court intervened and stay the operation of the impugned order of the High Court of Gauhati (Shillong Bench) dated 12 June 1987, in Civil Rule No.424 of 1975. The petitioner, further prayed the Hon'ble Supreme Court to issue an injunction restraining the respondent from preventing interfering with the business of traders of Bara Bazar, Shillong, which they had been doing since several years. The petitioner also prayed to pass an ad-interim ex-parte order in terms of prayers as well as to pass such other orders as the Hon'ble Supreme Court deems fit and proper.[104]

In giving judgement and decisions, the Hon'ble Supreme Court did not entertain much on the case, since the petitioner did not press much on the appeal petition. Therefore, the Hon'ble Justices, Mr. O. Chinnappa Reddy and Mr. K. Jagannatha Shetty of the Supreme Court, after hearing the learned counsel dismissed the special leave petition and the judgement was in favour of the respondent. The judgement was delivered on 26 August 1987.[105]

Notes and References

1. Compilation from District Council's Office files.
2. The term *Elaka* refers to any administrative unit in the District or any other administrative unit to be constituted and declared as such by the Executive Committee as per the United Khasi-Jaintia Hills Autonomous District (Appointment and Succession of Chiefs and Headmen) Act, 1959. Each *Elaka* corresponds to a *Syiemship, Lyngdohship, Sirdarship* and *Wahadadarship.*
3. "Ka jingmudui pyrshah ïa u Mr. X, Z Village ba u la wan pynjot ïa ka ïing jong nga u Mr. A ha ka 31.8.84 (Sngi Pomtiah)", Ha ki Secretary and Member, bad ki Riewkhmat bad ka Dorbar Z Village dated 3.9.84. (A letter from Mr. A, Headman, dated W Village, 3rd September 1984, about a complaint against Mr. X, Z Village, for he had come and damaged my house, Mr. A, on 31.8.84).
4. A letter from the Secretary, Z Village along with the Chairman, and others to the Sirdar of Marbisu, Marbisu Sirdarship, dated 25.9.84.
5. Office of the *Sirdar* of Marbisu, Marbisu *Sardarship,* dated Marbisu, the 27th September 1984.
6. Office of the *Sirdar* of Marbisu, Marbisu *Sirdarship, Enquiry,* dated 2 October 1984.
7. Ka Rai Dorbar u Sordar bad ki Paidbah W Village la long mynta ka sngi 13.10.84 (The decision of the *Sirdar* and

his *durbar* along with the inhabitants of the W Village was held today the 13.10.84), p.1.

8. *Ibid.*

9. Since the judgement of the Village Court, Marbisu village was not very clear, whether the complainant could get any compensation for the damage caused to his house. In an interview with the ex-Secretary of the Village Court. Mrs. Dramon Kurbah on 29 December 1990, Mrs. Kurbah informed that out of a fine of Rs.300/- paid to the *Sirdar* of Marbisu by the defendant, Rs.150/- was given by the *Sirdar* to the complainant, Mr. A as a compensation for damaging his house. In addition, a sum of Rs.300/- paid to the local *durbar* was utilised for the needs of the local village. Further, a *durbar* fee of Rs.20/- each paid by the complainant and the defendant were distributed Rs.10/- each to the members of the Village Court.

10. In the Village Court *Raid* Mawbuh, Umroi, Mylliem *Syiemship*, Ka Jingmudui Hok Dakhol jong ka Nongmudui halor ka Jaka Umshyngiar ba la thang ding da u Mr. C, ba la phah da ka Shahmudui, (A Plaint petition of the right to possession of the complainant over the land at Umshyngiar set fire by Mr. C as directed by the defendant), dated 25 June 1981, p.1.

11. *Ibid.*, pp.2-3.

12. Office of the Village Court Raid Mawbuh, Umroi, Mylliem *Syiemship, Civil Case No.1 of 1981, Pur. No.RM/C.C./1/81/188, dated Umroi, 25 June 1981.*

13. In the Village Court, Raid Mawbuh, Mylliem *Syiemship*, Umroi, *Civil Case No.1 of 1981, Ka Rai,* (Judgement), dated 23 December 1985, p.3.

14. *Ibid.*, p.4.

15. *Ibid.*, pp.6-12.

16. *Ibid.*, pp.6-7.

17. *Ibid.*, p.8.

18. *Ibid.*, pp.8-10.

19. *Ibid.*, pp.10-11.
20. *Ibid.*, p.12.
21. This case was appealed by the complainant to the court of the *Syiem* of Mylliem *Syiemship*, Shillong, on 20 February 1986, vide Title Civil Appeal No.1 of 1986. On 31 August 1989, the Additional Subordinate District Council Court, Mylliem *Syiemship* transferred the case to the Judge of the District Council since the Acting *Syiem*, Mr. Armstrong Syiem cannot try the case. The Judge of the District Council Court by his order dated 11 November 1989, transferred the case to the Khyrim *Syiemship*, Smit, on 1 December 1989, as Misc. Appeal No.1 of 1989. The Court of the Khyrim *Syiemship*, Smit, treated the case as Misc. Case No.5 of 1989.
22. Ha ka Additional Subordinate District Council Court, Mylliem *Syiemship*, Mawkhar, Shillong. "Ka Jingmudui ban pynbha ïa ka Jinglonghok Jinglongtrai, ban khang shipor bad ban pynmih", U Nongmudui, (A plaint petition of the right of ownership and to vacate the land), Complainant, dated Shillong, 19th May 1978, Suit No.4 of 1978, p.1.
23. *Ibid.*, pp.1-3.
24. Ha ka Additional Subordinate District Council Court, Mylliem *Syiemship*, Mawkhar, Shillong, Ka Jubab Jingthoh Jong ki Shahmudui No.1 & 2, Suit No.4 of 1978, Ki Shahmudui (A written statement of the defendant No.1 & 2), dated Shillong, the 29th August 1978, pp.1-2.
25. *Ibid.*, pp.2-4.
26. In the office of the Additional Subordinate District Council Court, Mylliem *Syiemship*, Issues, Suit No.4 of 1978, p.24.
27. Office of the Additional Subordinate District Council Court; Mylliem *Syiemship*; Shillong, Suit No.4 of 1978, Ka Rai (Judgement), dated 10.4.82, pp.2-4.
28. *Ibid.*, pp.2-3.
29. *Ibid.*, p.3.

30. *Ibid.*
31. *Ibid.*, p.4.
32. *Ibid.*, p.3.
33. *Ibid.*, p.4.
34. This case was appealed by the defendants (Plaintiff) to the Court of the Judge, Khasi Hills District Council Court, Shillong, on 19 July 1984, vide Title Civil Appeal No.4 of 1984, which had dismissed the appeal as per judgement of the Court on 22 April 1985.
35. Office of the Additional Subordinate District Council Court, Mawphlang *Lyngdohship*, Mawphlang, Civil Suit No.4 of 1974, Ka Jingïasaid: Ki Khmat, (Gist of Argument), dated 21 January 1978, p.1.
36. In the Court of the Additional Subordinate District Council Court, Mawphlang, Ka Jubab Jingthoh jong u Mr. P, Shahmudui No.1 (A written statement of Mr. P, the defendant No.1), dated 25 March 1975, pp.1-2.
37. *Ibid.*, Ka Jubab Jingthoh jong ki Co-defendants No.2, 4 & 5 (A written statement of the Co-defendants No.2, 4 & 5), dated 25 March 1975, p.1.
38. Office of the Additional Subordinate District Council Court, Mawphlang *Lyngdohship*, Mawphlang, Civil Suit No.1 of 1974, Ka Rai (Judgement), dated 29 April 1978, p.3.
39. *Ibid.*, pp.3-7.
40. *Ibid.*, p.5.
41. *Ibid.*, pp.4-5.
42. *Ibid.*, p.7.
43. This decision was appealed by the complainant to the court of the judge, Khasi Hills District Council Court, Shillong, on 4 May 1978, vide Title Civil Appeal No.7 of 1978, directed against the information by the trial court dated 29 April 1978, which accordingly dismissed the appeal as per judgement of the court dated 17 September 1979. On 25 April 1981, the petitioner (MS.A.) filed a

petition before the court of the judge for execution of the Decree vide Misc. Case No.13 of 1981, which accordingly passed the Execution Order as per Judgement declared on 28 August 1981. The opposite party (MS.Q) on 26 June 1982, preferred a Civil Revision vide Civil Revision No.3 of 1982, directed against the execution order dated 19 August 1981, which revision was allowed as per judgement of the court dated 7 December 1983.

44. Ha ka Additional Subordinate District Council Court, Mawdon *Sirdarship*, Title Civil Appeal No.1 of 1983, Ka Dorkhast Appil (Appeal petition), dated 28 November 1983, p.1.

45. XY Village Court, XY, Title Suit No.1 of 1981, Ka Rai (Judgement) No.1 of 1983, dated XY, the 20th October 1983, pp.1-7.

46. Ha ka Additional Subordinate District Council Court, Mawdon *Sirdarship*, Appeal No.1 of 1983, Ka Rai (Judgement) ba la pynmih ha ka 20th March 1984 (Judgement decided on 20th March 1984), p.6.

47. *Ibid.*, p.9.

48. *Ibid.*

49. *Ibid.*

50. *Ibid.*, pp.7-9.

51. *Ibid.*, pp.9-10.

52. *Ibid.*, p.10.

53. The case was appealed by the appellant to the Court of the Judge, Khasi Hills District Council Court, Shillong, on 16 May 1984, vide Title Civil Appeal No.1 of 1983, directed against the judgement dated 20th March 1984, which accordingly quashed the appeal as per judgement of the Court, T.C.A. No.3 of 1984, dated 19th March 1986.

54. Additional Subordinate District Council Cout, Wahadadar Shella Confederacy, Misc. Case No.11 of 1978, Ka Dorkhast Jong u Nongai Dorkhast (Plaint petition of the Complainant), dated 24 December 1979, pp.1-2.

55. *Ibid.*

56. In the Additional Subordinate District Council Court, Wahadadar Shella Confederacy, Misc. Case No.11 of 1979, Ka Rai (Judgement), No.8 of 1980, p.3.

57. *Ibid.*, pp.3-4.

58. After the decision, the claimant filed another Misc. Case No.11 of 1980, for evicting Ms. M and Mr. G of L who continued to stay in the shop.

59. In the Court of the Judge, District Council Court, Shillong, Misc. Criminal Case No.1 of 1987, Petition U/S 125 Cr.P.C. Humble Petitioner (Ka C of M Village), dated 22nd April 1987, pp.1-2.

60. In the Court of Mr. JN, Magistrate 1st Class, Subordinate District Council Court, Shillong, Misc. C.R. Case No.1 of 1987, Judgement, dated 17th June 1988, pp.2-5.

61. *Ibid.*, pp.3-5.

62. *Ibid.*, p.3.

63. *Ibid.*, pp.3-4.

64. *Ibid.*, p.4.

65. *Ibid.*, pp.4-5.

66. *Ibid.*, p.5.

67. The case was appealed by the opposite party to the Court of the Judge, Khasi Hills District Council Court, Shillong, on 26 August 1988, vide Criminal Revision No.1(A) of 1988, directed against the judgement dated 17 June 1988, which had disposed of the appeal as per judgement of the Court on 15 May 1989.

68. Ha ka Additional Subordinate District Council Court: Khyrim *Syiemship*, Smit, Misc. Case No.7 of 1988, Ka Dorkhast pan hukum khang shipor katkum ka Spirit Ka 0.39 r. 1 bad C.P.C., dated 2nd August 1988, pp.1-2.

69. Additional Subordinate District Council, Khyrim *Syiemship*, Smit, Misc. Case No.7 of 1988, Ka Hukum (Order), dated Smit, the 27th February 1989, pp.1-2.

70. u C D & Others (Appellants), An Appeal under Rule 29 of the Khasi Hills Autonomous District (Administration of Justice) Rules, 1953, and as amended upto date against the Order dated 27.2.89 passed by the Presiding Officer, Addl. Subordinate District Council Court of Khyrim Syiemship at Smit in Misc. Case No.7 of 1988, dated 7 April 1989, pp.1-3.
71. In the Court of the Additional Judge, Additional District Council Court, Khasi Hills, Shillong, Misc. Appeal No.1 of 1989, Judgement, dated 16 November 1989, pp.1-3.
72. *Ibid.*, pp.2-3.
73. *Ibid.*, p.2.
74. *Ibid.*, pp.2-3.
75. *Ibid.*, p.3.
76. *Ibid.*
77. *Ibid.*
78. In the Court of the Judge, District Council Court Khasi Hills, Shillong, Divorce Suit No.8 of 1988, in the matter of an application for dissolution of Marriage, Petitioner (Mrs. M B), dated 9th September 1988, pp.1-2.
79. *Ibid.*, p.3.
80. *Ibid.*
81. Before the Judge, District Council Court, Khasi Hills, Shillong (Matrimonial Court of Original Jurisdiction), Divorce Suit No.8 of 1988, Judgement, dated 10th July 1989, p.2.
82. *Ibid.*
83. *Ibid.*, pp.2-3.
84. Petition of the Petitioner, u Jidon Singh Syiem, Syiem of Langrin, dated 17 December 1980, p.1.
85. *Ibid.*, pp.2-3.
86. Office of the Executive Committee, Khasi Hills District Council, Shillong, Order of the Executive Committee in

the matter of the prolong illness of u Doli Singh Syiem, the Syiem of Langrin Syiemship vis-á-vis the administration of the Elaka, dated the 24th October 1980, p.18.

87. Office of the Executive Committee, Khasi Hills District Council, Shillong, Notification No.DC.XXVII/47/PF/Gen/80/44, Shillong, the 25th October 1980.

88. In the Gauhati High Court (High Court of Assam, Nagaland, Meghalaya, Manipur and Tripura), Civil Rule No.629 of 1980, Judgement, dated 6 May 1981, pp.7-12.

89. *Ibid.*, pp.9-12.

90. In the Supreme Court Judgement it states that the authorities concerned would at all relevant times have the power to appoint or remove administrative personnel under the general power of administration vested in them by the Sixth Schedule. The view taken by the High Court that there could be no appointment or removal by the District Council without a law having been first passed in that behalf under paragraph 3(1)(g) cannot be sustained.

91. F.n. 169, p.7.

92. *Ibid.*

93. *Ibid.*, pp.7-8.

94. *Ibid.*, p.9.

95. *Ibid.*

96. *Ibid.*, pp.9-10.

97. *Ibid.*, pp.10-11.

98. *Ibid.*, pp.11-12.

99. *Ibid.*, p.12.

100. In the Supreme Court of India, Civil Appellate Jurisdiction, Civil Leave Petition (Civil) No.8394 of 1987, New Delhi, Petition of the Petitioner, dated July 1987, pp.4-6.

101. *Ibid.*, pp.7-8.

102. In the Gauhati High Court (The High Court of Assam, Nagaland, Meghalaya, Manipur, Tripura, Mizoram and Arunachal Pradesh), Shillong Bench, Civil Rule No.424 of 1975, Judgement and Orders, dated 12 June 1987, pp.14-15.

103. F.N. 100, pp.9-14.

104. In the Supreme Court of India, Civil Appellate Jurisdiction, Civil Miscellaneous Petition No.8395 of 1987 in Special Leave Petition (Civil) No.8394 of 1987, dated August 1987, pp.1-3.

105. Supreme Court of India (Record of Proceedings), Court No.2, Item No.8, Section XIV, Order, dated 26 August 1987.

9
CONCLUSION

The Khasis had their deep-rooted tribal institutions since time immemorial. At the beginning, the power of the village council seemed to be unlimited because it exercise sovereign powers within the areas of the jurisdiction. But with the evolution of the confederacies of village or *Raid* and the final evolution of the *Hima* or State most of the powers of the village council were taken away by the higher authorities and the village council lost all its sovereign powers. When the British assumed sovereignty over the land these indigenous organisations were not swept away. The British took advantage of this existence and the authority of the *syiems* were recognised through *sanads* granted by the sovereign power. The *sanad* ratified the appointment of the *syiem* on his election and he was subject to the control of the Deputy Commissioner of the District of Khasi and Jaintia Hills. Traditionally, the *syiem* is not the head of the state but he is a nominal head. He is the symbol of unity and integrity of the State. It is the *Dorbar Hima* which is the paramount power. It was during the British rule that paramount power was taken away from the *Dorbar Hima*. The British Government as the paramount power reserved to itself the right to remove the *syiem* in case of oppression or misconduct or dereliction of duty.

After the lapse of a British paramountcy, the twenty five Khasi States formed a federation of their own as the 'Federation of Khasi States' and acceded to the Dominion of India subject to the provisions of an agreement by means of an Instrument of Accession. By this instrument, although the *syiems* acceded to the Dominion of India they did not liquidate their separate entity and resolved to maintain their old-age customs and usages regarding the administration of Khasi States, election of chief or Headmen, power of *Dorbar*, etc. All these changes leave far reaching consequences.

In Khasi Hills the system of administration of justice was fascinating. For a long time, the administration was carried on according to customary law. The Codes of Civil and Criminal Procedure were not introduced into the Khasi Hills. But the spirit of these codes was observed by the administrator. Under the British Raj the rulers of the Khasi States were empowered to govern their respective States and allowed to adjudicate and decide all civil and criminal cases except the more heinous ones in which their own subjects alone were concerned through *Sanads*. Later, during the time of the Province of Assam their powers were retained with modifications and accordingly they were empowered to adjudicate and decide all civil cases and all criminal offences, except those punishable with death, transportation or imprisonment for five years and upwards which may arise within the State in which the parties were Khasis.

Further, the Governor of Assam in 1937 framed Rules for the administration of justice and police in the Khasi and Jaintia Hills in exercise of power under Section 6 of the Scheduled Districts Act, 1874, for the British areas of

Shillong and the 31 British *Sirdarships* in the Khasi Hills district, but not for the non-British area. The administration was vested in the Governor of Assam, Commissioner, Deputy Commissioner and his assistants and the traditional village authorities recognised by the Government. When the Assam High Court was established in 1948, the judicial authority was transferred to this Court. The said Rules, however, were not applicable in the Shillong administered areas in as much as the area comprised within the *Hima* (State) of Mylliem. This judicial authority was still retained and recognised even upto the eve of the Indian Independence as per agreement accepted by the Governor General of India on 17 August 1947. On the other hand, the Khasi States continue to exercise the judicial authority with little modifications under the Khasi States (Application of Laws) Order, 1948, and the Khasi *Syiemship* (Administration of Justice) Order, 1950, which applies to the Khasi States excluding so much of the areas comprised within the Municipality of Shillong.

On the coming into existence of the District Council, the judicial powers in the autonomous area of United Khasi and Jaintia Hills Districts, the Khasi people were governed by the United Khasi-Jaintia Hills Autonomous District (Administration of Justice) Rules, 1953, framed by the United Khasi-Jaintia Hills Autonomous District Council. On its coming into force, the *syiems* exercise their powers under the said District Council Rules and the Administration of Justice Rules, 1950, and 1952, were repealed by Rule 58 of the said Rule of 1953 in so far as they related to the matters dealt with the 1953 Rules. The *Syiem's* Courts and the District Council's Court exercises judicial power and jurisdiction over all the Shillong Administered Areas except the areas comprised in the Shillong Municipality only as amongst the tribal people. Since the existence of the District Council and after the enactment of the said Rules of 1953, different courts were set up in the KHADC. The Judge of the District Council Court has equivalent powers like the District and Session Judge and the District Council Magistrate has also sentencing powers of five to seven years as has been offered upon them by the Governor's order under Paragraph 5 of the Sixth Schedule to the Constitution of India.

The analysis of the system of administration of justice in Khasi Hills shows that the Courts set up at different levels by the KHADC have control over the administration of justice in their respective areas. No doubt, the KHADC Court is carried out by legal experts and judicial officers having degrees in law on the trial of cases, disputes efficiently and expeditiously. Of course, judicial autonomy of the hills is often abused. Money economy has further aggravated the deteriorating condition of the utility and importance of the tribal system of justice. Oaths whether of traditional or of modern forms are not always reliable. Influence can lead to misinterpretation of the tribal customary laws. It is, therefore, necessary that judicial uniformity be introduced for the administration of justice. But there are almost insurmountable difficulties in bringing about this judicial uniformity. The difficulties arise out of the fact that nowhere in the hill areas customary laws have been codified. Although in Khasi Hills, Khasi laws that were partially codified by the Khasi National Durbar in 1925 and served as the basis of Sir Keith Cantlie's *Notes on Khasi Law* have not been found uniformly applicable and were objected to by the articulate non-Christians.

Since the customary laws are not codified and uniformly interpreted, the introduction of a uniform system of justice seems to be very difficult. The Khasi people do not feel enthusiastic in codifying their customary laws at present. With the existence of the autonomous District Councils, the thrust seems to be more on legislation rather than codification. Codifications will naturally encourage litigations. Legislations, no doubt, can provide for a sort of uniformity in their traditional system rather than codifying the customary laws that vary from *Elaka* to *Elaka*. Thus the question of codification and uniform interpretation of the customary laws of the Khasi people needs immediate attention to bring into existence a uniform system of administration of justice in their respective *elakas* and thereby to avoid misinterpretation or their being influence by certain sections.

As the Pataskar Commission commenting on judicial autonomy said,

> "The expectation in the beginning was that the district councils would continue the age-old methods of the tribal people to dispense justice in an inexpensive and simple manner as the tribal people had been doing in the past. Instead we find that the District Councils have established a hierarchy of courts very much akin to the set up in the other parts of the State .... We believe, the Councils can ill afford .... the sophisticated judicial processes and modern laws would still be alien to the tribal society in its present stage of development. The full impact of modern judicial administration will create difficulties for the tribal people and add to administrative complexities in these areas....There is to our mind no harm and a good deal of advantage in allowing the tribals to continue to administer justice through their simple procedure."[1]

The basis of administration of justice in Khasi Hills has been simple and inexpensive. But due to the introduction of modern legal system to that of the Khasi traditional system, the Khasis have failed to get the best of the two systems. Only the well-to-do people in the Khasi society have benefitted out of this confused system of judicial administration.

The Dutta Commission's report of enquiry appointed by the State Government on the functioning of the District Councils in Meghalaya has rightly pointed out:

> "the District Councils have practically no machinery to enforce their laws and orders. For example, the Village Court set up by the district council has no means to compel the attendance of an accused before it. Whenever, the Village Court wrote to the district authorities for the arrest of an accused, they treated the letter as an FIR and got the accused arrested, but had produced him in the Deputy Commissioner's Court and not the Village Court."[2]

After the District Councils have set up the Courts, all the cases involving non-tribal people are tried exclusively by the courts under the Deputy Commissioner which also try cases relating to offences, punishable by death, imprisonment for life or for a term of not less than five years, even though they may involve tribal people, till a court under the District Councils are empowered by the Governor to try such cases. In the KHADC, it is found that the Courts have been invested with this power. But in most cases, only the tribal people are involved. In this respect, mention may be made that according to the Pataskar Commission it was stated that:

> "…. the organisations of the tribal people which have advocated the extension of the jurisdiction of the District Council Courts over non-tribals supported their proposal on the ground that the inability of these Courts to try cases relating to non-tribals, 'Wounds the Sentiments' of the tribal people."[3]

As such, it is, therefore, felt that the jurisdiction of the District Council Courts should also be extended to the non-tribal people. It is also strongly felt that non-tribal people should not be subjected to the jurisdiction of the Courts of the Council if the cases involve between the tribal and non-tribal people.

Notes and References

1. Government of India, Ministry of Home Affairs, *Report of the Commission on the Hill Areas of Assam 1965-66* (Government of India Press, New Delhi, 1966), pp.101-102.
2. See, "Dutta Commission Report Forewarns: District Councils will die a Natural Death", *Shillong Times*, Vol.XLV, No.29, dated 13 September 1989, p.2.
3. Fan. 1, p.101.

INDEX